My Antiques Journey

BILL D'ANJOLELL

Table of Contents

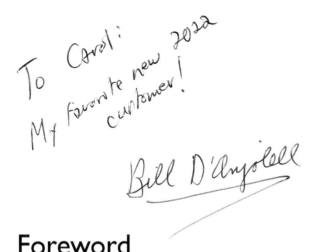

To Carol:
My favorite new 2022
customer!

Bill D'Angelell

Foreword

This is an autobiographical, behind-the-scenes look at one antiques dealer and appraiser. The first part deals with my youth and family. The second part is my introduction to antiques, the people I've met along the way, and my valentine to the Bucks County Antiques Dealers Association. The last part is like a reference section in the Philadelphia area, including where to find excellent antiques, where to find the best auction houses, how to downsize your home, a peek behind the scenes of an antiques show, and what's selling and what's not.

There are moments in our lives that we wished lasted longer and there are moments we wished never happened. I captured some of both.

It has been said that to be an antiques dealer involves being a little bit "crazy." This is very true in the age of the internet, which makes selling in retail stores and antiques shows very uneven and sometimes dismal.

Some names were changed to protect the guilty.

Introduction

Getting involved in the antiques business was an easy transition for me because of my love of history and old architecture. Attending Rider College back in the late 1970s to early 1980s, before it became a university, I majored in Management and Organizational Behavior. This major was an interesting combination of management, marketing, and psychology courses. Rider University, which has a national reputation, started in 1875 as a business school.

While attending Rider, I would frequent a nearby bustling flea market in Lambertville, New Jersey, called the Golden Nugget. It's open Wednesdays, Saturdays, and Sundays. Carrying my parents' unwanted things from home, I would sell them at the flea market to make extra money. It was also here that my love of history met up with discovering antiques. At the time, I never realized it would become a vocation for me. It was just fun listening to the old curmudgeons spin their tales and hunting for those vintage things everyone remembered their grandparents once owned.

I collect vintage books on Teddy Roosevelt and Arthur Conan Doyle, Beatles memorabilia, and Philadelphia Phillies yearbooks. I started collecting those yearbooks when I was a kid with the help of my father, who took me to my first Phillies game in 1964 at the old Connie Mac Stadium. The ballpark was starting to show its age by the time I first saw a game there. Parking was also difficult, but a new ballpark, Veterans Stadium, was still six years away from finished construction. However, the excitement of the fans, the salty smell of the hot dogs, the fresh scent of the grass field, and the uproarious rooting for the home team left an indelible impression on my young mind. I was hooked.

When you are a collector, the hunt and the discovery of that desired special item is always intriguing.

A 1951 Phillies yearbook, the rarest of all Phillies yearbooks, in mint condition, is worth $400.

CHAPTER 1

My Parents: When Bill Met Gerri

My father, William D'Anjolell, Jr., grew up in West Philadelphia in a beautiful predominately Italian, Jewish, and African-American neighborhood. Most of the homes were large, stone three-story buildings, including the twin homes. There was a trolley that went down 63rd Street where my father lived. On some corners there were little islands of grass, flowers, and shrubs that shared the neighbors' attention and care. It was a gorgeous and wholesome neighborhood in which to grow up.

My father went to Overbrook High School, where his younger brother, Bob, and younger sister, Jean, followed. My Aunt Jean was actually in a class with future superstar basketball player Wilt Chamberlain, who she said was a nice, quiet young man.

Years later a Wilt Chamberlain 1961 Philadelphia 76ers signed jersey sold for $17,000.

My great-grandfather, Louis D'Anjolell, was an orphan, born in Nice when it was part of Italy. In the mid to late nineteenth century, the border for Nice would change between France and Italy all the time. Today, with Nice, France, being so close to the border, most of the people there speak both languages. Louis, being an orphan, was placed in an Italian military school. A good student, he learned to speak seven languages. At the turn of the century, he came to America with his wife and they eventually had two girls and three boys—Gina, Leticia, Norman, Roland, and my grandfather, William. Louis worked various jobs, and with his knowledge of languages he later worked in the World Court making a good salary as a translator. The World Court is the principal judicial organ of the United Nations (UN). It settles legal disputes between member states and gives advisory opinions to authorized UN organizations and specialized agencies. It was founded in 1945, just after World War II. At the dinner table, Louis said, "We will speak English because it's the language of our adopted country." I admired him for that. He also talked about the fine homes he had been invited to and their extraordinary furnishings. He died a couple years after I was born. I wish I had had a chance to know him.

A French Baccarat crystal chandelier with twelve arms and lights, circa 1900—around the time my great-grandfather came to America—is worth $78,000.

My grandfather, William D'Anjolell, Sr., was included in a business with his two brothers Norman and Roland for a while, but I think it became a case of "too many chiefs and not enough Indians." Norman and Roland were snappy dressers, especially Uncle Roland, who could walk out of GQ magazine, while my grandfather wore good quality but very loud suits, shirts, and ties. You needed a volume control button on his clothes.

A 1930 to 1940 Swank gold-tone tie clip chain with charm is worth $15.

Later, William owned a beer distributorship on Lebanon Avenue in Philadelphia, not far from his home. His store was popular with the local colleges because he carried imported hard-to-find products like Carlsberg Beer from Denmark.

My father worked there in his twenties while attending LaSalle College. It wasn't the easiest job. In the 1950s, there weren't any cans of beer—only glass bottles. Canned beer wasn't invented yet. During the day, he would need to bring stock up from the basement. He carried two or three cases of beer at a time, making his way slowly up the narrow steps. Hanging from my own basement is the metal sign I inherited from the beer store that boasts our family name. More than a few antique dealers have asked to buy that sign, worth about $300. I don't care how much they offer—I'm not selling it. I recall being attracted to a 1960s Budweiser Clydesdale carousel ceiling light hanging inside my grandfather's store. It is worth about $1,200. I wish I knew where that was today.

My grandfather also rented out apartments, including a guest bedroom in the back of his own home when he lived on Wynnewood Avenue in Philadelphia. This bedroom was rented to Vince DiMaggio. He was the older brother of Joe and Dom. Vince played for the Phillies during the 1940s and was a power hitter who struck out a lot. Dom was a good hitter and great centerfielder for the Red Sox his entire eleven-year career. Joe was the superstar centerfielder for the Yankees. Vince became close to our family and was my Uncle Robert's sponsor for his confirmation at church.

A Vince DiMaggio hand-signed autograph is worth $70, a Dom DiMaggio hand-signed autograph is worth $100, and a Joe DiMaggio hand-signed autograph is worth $350. All three brothers' signatures on a baseball is worth $2,300.

The nearby barber liked to tell the story about the time my grandfather was waiting for a delivery truck one afternoon. In front of his store on the street were painted white lines with the words, "No Parking/Delivery Zone." A man drove up and parked his van right on that spot. My grandfather came outside, and in a reasonable tone said,

"Could you please park down the street a little? I have a beer truck coming soon for a delivery."

The man said, "No."

My grandfather again asked politely. The man snarled, "No, you dirty wop!"

My grandfather said, "One moment."

You need to understand that my grandfather never followed any sports nor cared to have the slightest interest in sports. He went inside his store and came out with a large baseball bat. He proceeded to enter the guy's van and smash anything and everything inside using his bat. With that, the owner started screaming, "He's crazy!"

My grandfather turned to him and replied, "I am crazy."

The police arrived. They all knew my grandfather because he donated a case of beer to the men in blue every Christmas. One policeman put his arm around my grandfather and said, "Now, Bill, you just can't go around damaging other people's property."

My grandfather acknowledged, "I know, I know, I shouldn't have done it."

Then the other cop screamed at the man, "Why did you park here? You were warned. Get your car out of here and I won't give you a ticket."

A rare occasion when my grandfather hit his breaking point and lost it.

My wife hears this story and says to me, "That's where you get your temper."

This was all witnessed by the barber. Whenever you need to know what happens in a neighborhood, ask the barber.

An antique working barber pole in excellent condition is worth $1,100.

My mother, Geraldine Giampietro, grew up in Northeast Philadelphia in a section called Tacony. In the nineteenth century, the famous Henry Disston created the world's largest saw company called the Keystone Saw Works. His products received the highest honors at the Philadelphia Centennial in 1876. Located in Tacony, his saws were used throughout the world.

Disston vintage saws today, depending on condition, size, and how intricate the carving of the wood handle is, may be worth between $50 and $500 each.

Disston, like many factory owners at the time (including Hershey), had a paternalistic view of his employees and built thousands of homes in Tacony for his workmen. These were the houses in which my mother and her neighbors lived. They included row homes, twin homes, and some old stately mansions with high ceilings built for upper management.

Around this same time, during the early twentieth century, many Italian immigrants worked on Hog Island for the World War I effort to build ships that were mostly for cargo or troop transport. This is where the Philadelphia International Airport now sits. Italian American workers brought their lunch to work on Hog Island. Their lunch consisted of various meats, cheeses, and lettuce between two slices of bread. There was not a lot of time allocated for lunch so the European-style sandwich needed to be abbreviated into an Italian roll. This became known as the "Hog Island sandwich" or hoagie. Thus, the hoagie was born.

Many places make great hoagies, but one of my favorites is the White

House in Atlantic City, New Jersey. They've been in business since 1946.

A White House regular Italian submarine hoagie costs $15. Worth every penny.

My mother went to Frankford High School along with most of her friends. She played the piano and enjoyed music a great deal, especially since her father, Jerry, was a musician by trade. Music played in the house all the time. When she was older, she met a guy named Bill at a club that played good jazz. She kept seeing him at all these clubs she liked and found they admired the same music. One evening, she was out on a date with singer/musician Buddy Greco at a piano bar. Bill knew she would be there and showed up. Buddy was not amused.

Sheet music from the 1920s through the 1950s is worth only $2 to $10 and must be in excellent condition. People who collect paper antiques (ephemera) are careful to buy items close to pristine condition.

Later, my father saw her at a club at the Jersey Shore and love smitten, went up to her and said, "You don't know this yet, but you're the girl I'm going to marry."

My mother replied with a laugh, "Get out of here."

Yet, a few weeks later, Bill and Gerri were engaged.

They once went to the 500 Club in Atlantic City. The place is famous because the owner refused to allow Dean Martin and Jerry Lewis to appear there unless they worked together. The owner, Paul "Skinny" Damato, declared, "They work better together with Dean singing and Jerry breaking his balls."

An act was born, and Martin & Lewis became one of the biggest acts in theaters, television, and movies during the late 1940s through 1950s.

A 1955 Martin & Lewis movie poster from the film You're Never Too Young *is worth $450.*

My father's family knew the owner of the 500 Club well. When my parents tried to see a Frank Sinatra show, it was sold out. As soon as the owner saw Bill and Gerri arrive, he produced a "table for two" and carried it into the room. Sinatra was singing from a bar stool with a small combo as accompaniment. They got the best seat in the house—ten feet from Sinatra.

"Old Blue Eyes," without a doubt, sang the soundtrack to my parents' life.

It's a matter of record that Sinatra knew members of the mob. When he was fired from MGM Studios for making a pointed joke at the expense of Louis B. Mayer, only the mob would hire him. He sang in Vegas, but it took getting the role and winning the Oscar for *From Here to Eternity* to put him back on top.

Frank Sinatra could be brutal to people he didn't like, but he did some wonderful deeds for people too. He paid for all of actor Lee J. Cobb's medical bills when he was destitute. Jerry Lewis liked to say on his Muscular Dystrophy Telethon that Frank gave more money away as Mr. Anonymous than anyone else. Sometimes he did use his name— hospital wings are named after him in Atlantic City and other places. For my parents, it was sad day when he died.

A 1954 TV Guide with Frank Sinatra on the cover is worth $195.

My parents were married in 1957. Their wedding photo evoked old fashioned, movie star good looks. This was about the same time my father was drafted into the navy. He was stationed in Jacksonville, Florida, so they moved to Florida and rented a little cottage near the base. Dad was an air-traffic controller on the USS Randolph

Parents wedding photo

aircraft carrier, while my mother was a dental assistant for the lo-cal dentist.

The carrier was on a mission to patrol the Mediterranean Sea. On a calm night, the water can look like a sheet of glass. One evening, a plane was coming in to land on the carrier and the instruments were failing; the air-traffic controller told the pilot to pull up, but it was too late. He crashed into the sea and perished. Another seaman was standing too close to the large bands that help jets take off. When the band snapped back, it cut the man in half. A total of three men died during this non-war cruise in the Mediterranean.

Because some sailors get into trouble in bars, when the carrier docked in many Mediterranean ports like Istanbul, Turkey, officers would not allow these sailors to leave the ship. If you're arrested in Turkey, the U.S. Navy cannot get you out of jail.

Dad in the Navy

My father did enjoy other ports like Naples, where he and his friends ate at some fine restaurants—a bit better than the meals on ship.

A year later, he was honorably discharged, and I was born. My parents decided to live in my mother's old home in the Tacony section of Philadelphia.

A vintage sterling silver U.S. Navy pin is worth $45.

CHAPTER 2

My Youth

As an only child, you would think I would have a quiet, maybe lonely upbringing. This couldn't be further from the truth. We always had relatives, friends, and neighbors over at the house. Food and people were the common denominator all the time, whether it was a holiday, birthday, wedding, or not, our house was busy.

Both of my parents are Italian American, and like a lot of my relatives, my mother could cook for ten people in an instant. My mother would get upset if someone used Italian sauce out of a jar. Of course, Italians call sauce "gravy." Mom loved to cook, and not just Italian dishes. She loved to make paella—which is a Spanish dish with chicken, shrimp, saffron rice, sausage, artichoke hearts, and other ingredients—that serves a large amount of people. It was said that for this dish, my Uncle Nick Badolato could be locked in a cave at the North Pole, yet he would still somehow make it to the house in time for dinner. He loved my mom's cooking, like most people.

At Thanksgiving, we always had a large group for dinner. My mother would make turkey stuffing from scratch. Some of my friends thought this was some sort of modern miracle that it didn't come from a box.

You were always welcome at our home. In the evening, Mom could have cake and coffee ready at a moment's notice for visitors.

A 1920s "Old Reliable Coffee" tin sign, 9 inches tall by 6 inches wide, is worth $360.

My friend Sammy Marzulli lived two doors down and was always over at our house listening to the Beatles or the Monkees as we did at his home. His mom, Barbara, was like a second mother to me because I saw her so often. Oreos and milk were the snack of the day as we would play air guitar to our favorite songs. Sammy's parents also went out together often with my parents to hear a band, eat at a restaurant, or go to a party.

A 1966 Beatles original Yesterday and Today Butcher *Cover album in pristine condition is worth $1,200.*

If my parents had a party, Sammy and I would listen from my second-floor bedroom to their mature funny stories.

Sam and I loved riding bikes all over Tacony. There wasn't much traffic back then in our northeast Philadelphia neighborhood.

A 1966 Schwinn Stingray bicycle sells for $1,400. Today, Schwinn or Huffy bikes from the 1960s in fair condition value in the hundreds of dollars and up.

My mother had close friends with whom she grew up, including Terri DiTanna, Eda Peterman, and Ginny Merando. All three lived in Tacony and were all very close to me. It's incredible how warm everyone was in this neighborhood.

Terri DiTanna had a son and daughter. Her daughter, Debbie, was two years older than I was, and I had the biggest crush on her. I think half the male population of the older students at our school did too.

Eda Peterman was my godmother and maybe the kindest person in the world. She had two sons and two daughters. Her son Billy was in my grade and was always quick and very funny. His older brother, Howie, and I were watching the Police television show *Adam-12* when we were young and he said to me very seriously, "This is a really good show."

Howie loved this show, and he eventually joined the Philadelphia Police force and worked his way up to become a homicide detective. He was very good and solved two difficult homicides that were televised on the show *Investigative Discovery* on the Discovery Channel. Howie narrated both shows. Most policemen in Philadelphia know who Howard Peterman is. He is a great guy who recently retired from the force.

An Adam-12 *metal lunchbox with thermos, circa 1972, is worth $145.*

Ginny Merando, at one time, lived next door to us and sometimes watched me as a toddler. She had four brothers and a sister; by 2019, they had all passed away except for Ginny. I was close to her younger brother Rudy because we both loved the Beatles. They were a big, devoted family. My very first job at thirteen years old was working at their small grocery store on Longshore Avenue in our neighborhood. The store sold a little bit of everything, including Italian water ice in the summer. The Merando patriarch was known as "Pop" to everybody. Like so many stores in the Tacony section of Philadelphia, it's no longer there.

A personalized vintage grocery store double-sided metal sign, circa 1960, is worth about $120.

My friends and I in this Italian, Irish, and Polish Catholic neighborhood attended Our Lady of Consolation School. The Sisters of St. Francis were the order of nuns who taught here, and they could be tough.

Yes, they did use the yardstick on our knuckles and rear ends—not something Catholic schools could enforce today. However, my first-grade teacher, Sister Helen Mary, was one of the finest educators in the school. I loved her patience with students, her endearing kindness, and her ability to make us understand her lessons.

We also had lay teachers like the delightful Ms. Janice Wloch and others, who drilled us with the three R's: reading, writing, and arithmetic. It seemed like we had to do book reports all the time but could choose almost any book we wanted. For me, that was nonfiction American historical books and biographies. I loved reading about previous war conflicts involving the United States. Reading about former presidents like Washington, Lincoln, and Teddy Roosevelt was always interesting. I was more engaged with history than any other subject in school. These stories jumped out at me, which made it much easier to write essays.

Today, I carry presidential memorabilia to sell, and these three presidents, George, Abe, and Teddy, are the top presidents whom customers desire most.

Bronze Abraham Lincoln bookends, circa 1930, are worth about $85. A Teddy Roosevelt funeral program is worth $120.

Back then, Saturday morning television was for kids. We loved to watch local television programs like Gene London and Sally Starr. Gene would show movies, read stories, and draw large storybook illustrations for his audience. I loved his show. Today, children's shows seem to lack the imagination and depth of these earlier programs.

Most of my friends didn't particularly love school, but we had each other and had fun whether it was riding bikes, watching movies, listening to music, playing sports, board games, or just hanging out.

During those hot summer days, we went to the movies at the old Merben Theater or the Mayfair Theater, which were both down the street from each other on Frankford Avenue. They each could easily hold about five hundred people. They had signs that told customers they were "air-conditioned." It was so cold inside these theaters you could hang meat from the ceiling like a Dietz & Watson packaging plant. Admission was fifty cents for anyone under eighteen years of age. The candy they sold stuck to your teeth, which freaked out my mother, the dental nurse. We loved the movies. Both theaters are gone today, just like my youth.

A 1966 Fantastic Voyage 32-inch by 42-inch movie poster with linen backing is worth $2,000.

To this day, because of my love of films, I'll have friends call me late at night to ask me, "Who was the actor that helped Paul Newman win his case in the film, *The Verdict?*" (Answer: Jack Warden).

How I remember this trivia makes no sense because I cannot remember people's phone numbers. My favorite film of all time is probably *To Kill A Mockingbird*. I think as parents; we all strive for the wisdom and strength of Gregory Peck's portrayal of Atticus Finch.

A 1960 first edition of To Kill A Mockingbird by Harper Lee, signed by the author, is worth $1,100.

I played on a Christian Youth Organization (CYO) basketball team as a starting guard and also played on a Police Athletic League (PAL) little league baseball team. One year, we won the PAL baseball championship. I still have that trophy.

A 1960s baseball or football metal trophy is worth about $30. Today, trophies like these are all in plastic, or they give out plastic medallions to keep the costs down for schools.

One summer, between seventh and eighth grade, I played on a CYO-type baseball team. The coach was Mr. Pellegrini. He had us race to see who was the fastest on the team, and I won. What was the purpose of this? The coach would have me pinch run for two different people in the same game to steal second base, which I did, but of course, this is illegal in baseball. All I wanted to do was play shortstop. The coach had me play all over the diamond—third base, second base, right field, and I pitched one inning of a game. But I was never shortstop.

A 1960s infielder "Ken Boyer" baseball glove is worth $50.

We all loved and followed our home teams, which included collecting baseball and football cards. I wish I still had my old cards today. It was great going to Connie Mac Stadium to watch the Phillies or Franklin Field to see the Eagles play.

A 1964 Phillies Yearbook, second edition, is worth about $90 today. I own every Phillies Yearbook since they started in 1949.

We all spent a majority of our time doing outdoor activities. No one knew what a "couch potato" was. Cell phones and computers were still far in the future.

The church and school sponsored a carnival every summer where my friends and relatives would enjoy the rides, the games, and the food. The food was always good. I especially liked the Pizza Fritte, which was fried dough sprinkled with powdered sugar. The white powdered sugar all over their faces always made it easy to tell which kids had just finished eating a Pizza Fritte.

One summer at the carnival, they had local television celebrity Sally Starr, who as usual, wore her cowgirl outfit complete with six guns. She had a local television show that showcased cartoons and the Three Stooges. My friends and I loved the Stooges but girls never understood the laughs. It must be a guy thing.

A Colt model 1911 handgun, circa 1918, in excellent condition is worth $3,500.

The 1959 original Three Stooges in Have Rocket Will Travel *full-size movie poster is worth $1,900.*

Looking back at those carnivals, I only remember them as entertaining. No kids were kidnapped, robbed, or harmed in any way. There were no crimes that I knew of. Everyone watched over the kids and everyone else. You felt safe. We were fortunate that it was a close community. I wouldn't trade those younger years in grade school at Our Lady of Consolation or those summers in Tacony for anything in the world. We didn't know we were making such great memories, we were just having fun.

A 1950s to 1960s cardboard church carnival poster is worth $60.

For a couple years, I was an altar boy at our church and never had a problem with any of the priests. There were many of them because we had six masses on Sunday and several throughout the week. Unlike today, Sunday mass back in the 1960s and 1970s was packed with parishioners. Occasionally, masses were standing room only. The Communion portion of the Mass alone took over ten minutes. Sadly, most young people today hardly attend church or any places of worship.

Today, the school at Our Lady of Consolation doesn't exist, only the church. I think about how this little first- through eighth-grade school formed the young minds that later became good lawyers, doctors, police officers, members of the armed services, teachers, tradesmen, and professionals—all upstanding citizens.

———◆———

My parents moved us to Bucks County, Pennsylvania. It seemed many of my friends also moved out of the city throughout the 1970s. I attended Council Rock High School starting in 1972. Those four high school years went fast.

Before I could drive, my good friend Greg Casiello would drive me and our other friends in one of his parents' cars. We listened to tunes everywhere we went and very loudly.

A vintage Pioneer Super Tuner under-dash cassette player, the hottest car stereo system at the time, is now only worth about $60.

When my mother asked, "Who's driving to the movies?" or "the Phillies game?"

I would say, "Greg," and she was happy he was the driver.

She admired Greg's manners so much that I could be going anywhere and it was fine. If I said, "We're going to Hell, but Greg's driving," she would say, "OK, then. Have a good time. Bring some lotion; it may get hot."

With my father working long hours, Greg taught me how to drive in his family's Chevy Camaro. Using this car, I passed the driving test on the first try and have Greg to thank for that. O, captain! My captain! He was also our hockey team's captain.

This period with my friends—Greg, Joe, Frank, Steve S., Eric, Mark, Steve E., Kenny, Scott, Rick, Mike, and others—was exciting. We were on the hockey team together (Council Rock Renegades), and it seemed we went everywhere as a group.

Our little clique, in two automobiles, went to the first outdoor JFK Stadium rock concert, featuring Yes as the headliner. However, Peter

Frampton stole the show. It was right before his well-known *Frampton Comes Alive* LP was released and later sold more than eleven million copies worldwide. Everybody had this double album. In the 1970s, if you moved to the suburbs, I think that album came with the house.

A Peter Frampton autographed copy of Frampton Comes Alive *LP, circa 1976, is worth $185.*

At the time, the drinking age in New Jersey was eighteen, and New Jersey was only ten minutes across the bridge. One late Saturday night in 1975, we were at a drab New Jersey bowling alley. I was at the bar watching a comedy show I had never seen before and thought to myself, "This is really funny." This new show was called *Saturday Night Live,* and we all felt it spoke to our generation with current hip musical guests. It was a show to tape on your VCR. For my parents' generation, it was the Steve Allen show. This show was ours. VHS and Beta videotapes are worth absolutely nothing today—a great idea that became worthless fairly quick.

A vintage Ebonite pearl green bowling ball is worth $50.

Council Rock High School was considered one of the best and most progressive in Pennsylvania. In my freshman year, we had an assembly and no one knew what it was about. To our surprise, we had the band The Guess Who perform for us in the gym. Everyone went nuts. There's a film of this event that made it to public television.

The 1970 Guess Who "American Woman" 33⅓ LP album is worth $18.

All of us had part-time jobs to keep gas in our cars but also to earn money to see bands at clubs in New Jersey, buy records, go on dates, go to the shore, buy more records, and buy food. I worked at the Gap, Joe and Mark worked at a Roy Rogers restaurant (where they both met their respective wives), Greg worked at his father's gas station,

Steve S. worked at McDonald's, Frank worked at a golf course, Steve E. worked at his uncle's bowling alley, and so on.

While working at the Gap, I met the girls from Sister Sledge who sang "We Are Family," a big hit in the 1970s. They were so kind, and they lit up the room with their smiles. Also, at the Gap, I met a very quiet Ted Nugent who was followed by a subservient pretty young girl carrying his coat. I guess she was his assistant.

Ted Nugent's 1968 Gibson "Byrdland" guitar is worth $100,000.

Our 1976 senior class trip to Disney World was a first for any Council Rock senior class, and it was momentous. God bless Mrs. Goldfield, my former freshman English teacher who put the whole trip together. Today, it seems like every senior class from every school on the East Coast is going to Florida to see Mickey.

A vintage, circa-1960 Mickey Mouse wind-up watch by Lorus is worth around $100.

My friends and I would occasionally journey to my grandmother's shore home in Brigantine, New Jersey—a beautiful house two blocks from the beach. At night, we traveled to some of the clubs in Wildwood and other shore towns.

In Somers Point, New Jersey, we encountered Gregory's Bar, which was famous for its "five beers for a dollar." The guys liked this bar because our money lasted much longer, although we had some short hitters in our group. Four beers and they were done. The glass tumblers were tiny for beer; hence, the bar didn't lose money on this promotion. What worried me was the unsanitary way they cleaned their glasses. I watched how the bartender would place the glass in a quick soapy water rinse and then lay it to dry. I'm not a germophobe, but somebody was going to get sick and it turned out to be me.

On the way back to our Brigantine home base, I yacked in the front seat of my friend Joe's car. I was terribly sick and don't remember how I entered the house or was put into bed. Later, I learned it was Joey D.—a great guy, a great dad, and a wonderful granddad who today has nine kids and eleven grandkids. God bless them.

A 1910 Roseville pottery child's bowl, 7.5 inches in diameter, is worth $50.

Near the end of high school, my parents were in a terrible car accident on an icy road near their home in the middle of winter. A young man was driving up a hill, and my parents were driving down from the opposite direction. The young man threw out his cigarette with one hand and used the window handle with the other, leaving no hands on the steering wheel. The guy's vehicle slid into my parents' car sideways, pushing in the driver's side mirror, which broke the driver's side window. The glass shattered all over my father's face and neck. He was in the hospital, and doctors needed to pick out the glass from his face and body. Luckily, my mother was fine. Dad had to have his teeth wired shut for a couple weeks and had to eat his food through a straw. You could barely understand him when he talked, yet he insisted on answering the phone when it rang, which was just too funny because it sounded like he was saying, "Nello nhat nuph." The person calling our home may have felt they were receiving an obscene phone call. Thankfully, Dad came out of this fine with no scarring and a teeth-wired-shut language all his own.

A 1920 steampunk dentist chair by the A.O. Aloe company is worth $150.

Fast forward years later, Greg Casiello now lives in Louisiana with his wife and family. He flew up to Pennsylvania for family reasons and met up with seven of the former Renegades for a mini-reunion. We had a sentimental great time. Looking forward till the next occasion. Greg paid for everyone's dinner and drinks. Oh Captain, my Captain. A great guy!

A 1997 Eric Lindros Philadelphia Flyers authentic Nike jersey is worth $120.

My senior prom was memorable for all the wrong reasons. My date on prom night was a smart, pretty girl from my graduating class named Elaine. The prom was wonderful, but the day after, we were meeting up with another couple to go to Great Adventure Amusement Park. That rainy Sunday morning, I drove to pick up Elaine and I hydroplaned the car, spinning 90 degrees until the back of the car slammed into a telephone pole, cracking the rear axle and the pole. In a matter of seconds, the car was totaled. Not my finest moment.

To make matters worse, I didn't use my mother's old Ford LTD. I used my father's very cool new Cutlass Supreme Oldsmobile company car, probably to impress the girl. My father arrived at the scene and was concerned for my well-being, but I knew the screaming would come later. One week later to the day my father explained to me how much heat he received from his company for a car I should have never driven. I was grounded and embarrassed, my back ached, and my parents had to pay for a new telephone pole.

A Cutlass F85 Parts catalogue (1964-1975) is worth $350.

————— ◆ —————

Our family was full of some real heroes who helped shape me to what I am today. I am thankful for all of them.

My great aunt Jenny Sorrendino was my grandmother Rose's younger sister on my mother's side. During the Korean War, she was an army major in charge of nurses in a MASH unit. Aunt Jenny was close to the action of the war and saw some horrible things during that time. She and her nurses would write letters home for wounded or critically injured soldiers to their families and take care of them in the makeshift mobile hospital. Nurses would simply hold a patient's hand as they lay there dying. She retired a full colonel in the late 1960s. Aunt Jenny is alive and well and loves to watch her beloved Phillies. Aunt Jenny is a hero to me.

My grandmother Rose helped raise me as a baby when my parents were both working several jobs. She was a kind-hearted woman. When she retired from working as a floor manager at Gimbel's department store after twenty years, she moved to Brigantine, New Jersey, full time. When my friends would come down the shore with me for several days in the summer, many times we would go to the "Brigantine Castle." This rested on a pier over the ocean until a horrific storm took it down. My grandmother treated all my friends like they were her grandsons, and they all appreciated her care and kindness. She loved working in her garden along the side of her house with her roses, hydrangeas, and rhododendrons. One year, her flower bed was voted as the prettiest in Brigantine. She was so proud of that certificate that she later framed. Next door was a family that hit some rough spells after the mother died suddenly. My grandmother would make the father and son meals on a semiregular basis. She would bring the meals to their house or invite them to eat at her home. She would do so much for so many people. For that, my grandmother Rose is a hero to me.

My cousin Bobby Badolato was one of four brothers, the youngest brother and a retired Philadelphia policeman who loves animals and owns several dogs. Bob would go to a pound and pick out the oldest, most unwanted dog in the group and give it love and a great home until its final days. He does this all the time. For that, Bob is a hero to me.

My grandfather on my mother's side, Jerry Giampietro, joined the army after the attack on Pearl Harbor. In 1944, while on night patrol in France, he was shot in the back by a German sniper. He was in the army hospital for a long time. The bullet affected his bile and internal organs. After he was discharged from the hospital, he was placed in the army band called the "Rhythm Rations" because he could play several instruments, saxophone being his favorite. There were instances he acted as bandleader. When they needed a bass player, he found an African American who played well, but he needed permission from his commander to do so. African Americans weren't integrated with white units until the Korean War. The commander said, "Yes, but don't publicize this." After the war, my grandfather still felt pain in his back but rarely complained about it while he played in various bands throughout the late 1940s through the early 1960s. He worked in a duo, trio, and combo, playing various clubs, bars, private parties, and restaurants. Everyone enjoyed his music. When he visited us at Sunday morning breakfast, he always gave me a Morgan silver dollar, which accumulated to a few hundred. Much later, I cashed these coins in to a reputable dealer to attain a larger down payment for a home after I was married. My grandfather died in 1966 after, finally succumbing to his war wound from more than twenty years earlier. I still have his Purple Heart pin. He is my hero.

My uncle Robert D'Anjolell, Sr., my father's younger brother, is a funeral director in Philadelphia who later branched out to several locations throughout the suburbs. When Walter Annenberg, former owner of *The Philadelphia Inquirer* and philanthropist died, his wife called my uncle and said, "I want the best funeral for my husband, and I know you're the best." His several Memorial Homes are the best around the city of Philadelphia. When the AIDS epidemic first started in the early 1980s, no one knew what it was. Funeral directors in the city were so afraid of it they wouldn't bury anyone with the disease. My uncle was the first because he believed everyone deserves a dignified funeral. After his action, all the other funeral directors followed his lead. My uncle is a hero to me.

My grandmother Edith, my father's mother, was a tough, no-nonsense, but very caring person. She lived to be in her nineties. My uncle Robert, known as Fritz, while running his funeral home, dabbled in the restaurant business. He owned an Italian restaurant in Bala Cynwyd, Pennsylvania, called Ristorante Michelangelo, an upscale fine dining establishment. My father helped with his wine list because Dad was in the liquor business and knew more about wine than anybody. Typical with restaurants, my uncle had problems with the chef, the management, and so on. For a period, my grandmother was cooking the meals in this restaurant, on her feet for hours because the temperamental chef quit.

My uncle Robert's wife, Eleanor, known as Bunny, was killed in a terrible car accident. Her daughter, Dana, was severely injured in the vehicle but survived. Aunt Bunny dying completely shook our whole family. It was traumatic for everybody, especially Dana, who was just a little girl. My grandmother nursed her back to health and helped raise her and her two brothers, Rob and Jimmy. For that, my grandmother Edith is a hero to me.

My father, mother, and I would go out to dinner from time to time at some very fine restaurants. When I was very young, people said I always behaved myself no matter how high-end the restaurant or wherever the location. There were times I was the only child in the place. On one occasion, there was a noise at another table. As we were eating dinner, a man was screaming at this woman, calling her some harmful names that I was too young to understand. I could tell my parents were getting very irritated while they were trying to eat their meal. After a couple minutes of this, this man called his dinner guest a "stupid Polock." Again, I didn't understand at my age what was going on, but I felt nervous because my father, at six feet two inches tall, stood up and headed for their table. He said something to this man, which I found out later was, "Be quiet or leave the restaurant now!" I do not have an ounce of Polish blood in my body, but what my father did was nothing short of heroic to me. My father had such integrity and always did the right thing in helping people. He gave some serious money to my mother's uncle when he lost his job to facilitate him and his family getting back on their feet. He gave his old Ford LTD, which was the size of a boat in the 1970s, to a friend who was downsized from his job, and his car had died about the same time. He was always a good person to his family and his friends, and all of them would express that. My dad is a hero to me.

A 1970, eight-cylinder, four-door Ford LTD in excellent condition is worth $8,000.

Not all heroes wear capes. All of these individuals and others mean a lot to me. I think they all played a role on how I look at the world.

CHAPTER 3

The 1980s

Right before my 1981 graduation from Rider College, my friend Steve Stratton and I visited our mutual, very close high school buddy, Frank Gregory, who had recently moved to the Richmond, Virginia, area for his new job. He graduated from the University of Kentucky with an engineering degree and achieved a plum position working for a company known for its advanced energy and environmental technologies. Interestingly, this was Frank's first job after he graduated and he never worked for any other company. He is now close to retirement.

For Steve and me, it was our first time in Richmond and we learned that the bars and clubs closed around 10:00 p.m., unlike today when they close at 2:00 a.m. like most states. We visited a couple clubs playing country rock music—not my favorite, but it was fun hanging with Frank and catching up. We only had a couple days.

We left the bar at 10:00 p.m., a little too inebriated. Frank took us to a burger joint that helps you get sober quickly with its infamous Western Burger. This sandwich is a greasy burger with a fried egg on top. If you want, you can order your burger "all the way"—which includes a pickle on the very top with a greasy bun keeping it all together. I ordered mine "all the way." And it truly does make you sober, although not great for your stomach.

As we received our order, I noticed an African American young man waiting on the side. He wasn't allowed to order until all twenty-some white people received their food first.

I was appalled, but right before I spoke out to the woman behind the counter to say, "He's next," Frank grabbed my shoulder and said, "Don't do it or we'll need to fight our way out of here."

I thought, this is Frank's neighborhood, so I'll abide by his wishes, but looking back on this, I felt sorry for this guy. I was naïve at age twenty-one, thinking the Civil War was over.

A Civil War-era Confederate Script Calvary Cuff Button is worth $550.

After graduating from college, I fumbled through some retail management jobs over several years trying to find that elusive better profession. I retained some good friends over these years—Chris Ducko, George Massina, and George Evanick. We were all about the same age, liked the same music, and enjoyed many of the same clubs including Club Zadar and the Havana in New Hope, Pennsylvania, City Gardens in a tough part of Trenton, New Jersey, and others.

Chris worked at the old Bamberger's store, George Massina worked in a music store called Listening Booth, and George Evanick worked for an investment firm in a tall office building next to the mall. I managed a retail clothing store called Chess King. We were all situated at Oxford Valley Mall in Langhorne, Pennsylvania.

My intrepid good friend Christopher Ducko was hardworking and helpful to everyone he knew. On one occasion, he and his brother

The author in New Hope, 1977

Ed helped my parents install a new ceiling light in the kitchen of their home. Chris, a great carpenter, and Ed, a great electrician, had a labor-intensive project with all the wiring in a tight attic, but they finished after a couple hours.

Chris always did difficult jobs like this for his family and friends. He was like the guy in *MacGyver,* accomplishing feats in tough situations. I was in his large wedding when he married Lucy, a wonderful woman. He was godfather to my oldest daughter. He was just a good guy who always helped so many others.

A vintage midcentury sputnik starburst brass ceiling light is worth $130.

Many years later, sadly, Chris died at age forty-nine from a rare ailment. The mourners were wrapped around the block of the funeral home. It was the appropriate number of people for a man who had done so much good and touched so many. This included the hockey team he coached whose young players wore their uniform jerseys to the funeral. He left behind his loving wife and three sons. He saved me from many jams. God bless you, my friend.

In the 1980s on a Saturday night, at Club Zadar in New Hope, George Massina, George Evanick, and I listened to the sounds of Depeche Mode, the Cure, the Smiths and New Order among other 1980s bands on a great sound system. We danced with women who had big hair, blue hair, or no hair. They were heady times. We would close Club Zadar at 2:00 a.m., and then across the street, on the corner, Karla's Restaurant would reopen for breakfast. We went there because we were too wide awake to go home. We loved this restaurant, with its interesting tiles spread out on the walls.

A vintage hand-painted Dutch porcelain tile with floral design is worth $60.

We also liked the Havana Restaurant in New Hope where they once made strawberry daiquiris with real strawberries instead of a mix— great summertime drink. They still make a "Day after Thanksgiving" sandwich, which is exactly what you think it would be including the cranberry sauce and stuffing, and it tastes delicious. They still have impressive bands and outside seating today.

A vintage majolica Thanksgiving turkey platter, 20 inches in length, is worth $80.

Favorite stores that no longer exist in New Hope included Spinsters Records with its great selection of music CDs and records. We loved Zoli clothing store. The girls who worked there would assert their love for Club Zadar and City Gardens, which we knew from their attire and the music booming out of the ceiling speakers of their store.

The Now and Then Shop, located near the bridge to Lambertville, New Jersey, had the usual tourist items like candles, posters, incense, and such, but also a fascinating variety of off-the-wall items including illegal promotional records and bootleg records that studios and artists did not want released. They were sometimes referred to as underground records.

For example, the Beatles had their *White Album* released in 1968. There was also a bootleg *Black Album*. Someone stole tapes of unreleased alternate versions of songs from that era and released this illegal record. The term "bootleg" means it's not legal to release the music because there is no consent by the owner of the copyright for the song. This album included George Harrison's "All Things Must Pass," which was destined to be on the *White Album* and was later nixed, only to turn up on George's greatest-selling solo album in 1970. The sound quality was usually horrible because it was not mixed and produced properly. However, these items fetch quite the sum of money from collectors. Most websites won't sell these albums because it's illegal.

This 33⅓ Black Album *sells on the black market for $200.*

City Gardens was a whole other world where I mostly saw bands that were New Wave and Punk. George Massina's band, the Shades, played here, performing mostly originals a few times. George was the best drummer I ever saw live. The Shades played Brothers Club in Mercerville, New Jersey, and also, with my help, performed at John & Peter's Place in New Hope as well. They opened for the Hooters and a few other local bands. They made a self-produced single. One record label was interested in signing them to a contract, but the label wanted to add strings to one of their songs. The lead singer and main songwriter, Bob DeStefano, refused, and that was the end of a possible major label signing. I saw the Shades play often, and they were a good, tight band, but like so many groups, they never made it to the big time.

A Hooters 33⅓ album Nervous Night *signed by all five band members is worth $100.*

One of the bartenders at City Gardens was a quiet, young Jon Stewart of *The Daily Show* fame. He had a crush on Martha Quinn, an original

VJ from MTV who visited there to see a band. Everyone else had a crush on her too.

The MTV 1985 second annual Video Music Awards Program Book is worth $150.

At City Gardens, you might run into a few skinheads, but the club showed some important bands before they made it big like the Ramones and Green Day. You would watch from afar the slam dancing, but mostly, you hoped your car was still parked in the lot when you left the building. It was a tough place where I once met a pretty girl who was into goth and dressed the part. She was always sad but liked the music there. She loved dancing to the song "She Sells Sanctuary" by the Cult. I did too. I always hoped she made it to the other side and found her way.

The Cult Love CD featuring "She Sells Sanctuary" circa 1985 is worth $13.

George Massina's friend Fran was a very amiable guy I would run into on occasion. As a talented keyboard player, he wrote commercial jingles and moved to Nashville. His company performed backing tracks for Major League Baseball and National Football League promotions. Fran previously played with Alex Chilton. Alex was the former lead singer and guitarist for the band the Box Tops, who had a major hit song called "The Letter" back in the late 1960s.

George had not seen Fran since his move to Nashville, and when he returned for a visit, George said, "Whoa, you're wearing a big rug."

"No, George. It's a whole . . . hair . . . system," Fran explained quietly.

George shouted, "What do you mean? It's a hair piece!"

"No. It's a whole . . . hair . . . system," he insisted, a little louder.

"You're scaring me. I think it moved."

"It's a **whole . . . hair . . . system,**" Fran yelled, turning a little red in the face.

Everyone knew what he had. Despite Fran's obvious hairpiece, he would never concede its existence no matter how George prodded him. It did not detract from Fran's talent nor his success in the music business.

George is currently in the band the Characters. Their lead singer, Danny Solazzi, can handle vocals on songs from the 1960s through the 1980s. This band has backed Ray Manzarek of the Doors, three of the Monkees, Shirley Jones singing Partridge Family songs, actress Julie Newmar, and others. They're an excellent band that shines playing these older songs.

A 1966 Monkees toy guitar MIB (mint in box) is worth $385.

If we wanted to mellow out, we sat in the sofa pit area near the bar at the back of The Swan Hotel and restaurant in Lambertville. My friend Frank Adamski liked the relaxing back bar where they made the best Long Island Iced Teas. They are smooth at first and quite strong at the end. I always admired the back bar's long brass countertop and old-fashioned brass cash register. Years ago, on Sunday evenings, they had a piano player singing old World War I patriotic songs like "Over There." The music fit the venue.

A 1910 Lambertville postcard is worth $8 to $15.

My friend George Evanick was best man in my wedding. One night, he and his buddy both rode his motorcycle together to a bar in New Hope on Bridge Street. They closed the bar at 2:00 a.m. and went to leave. A waiting police officer outside told George's friend that he didn't think he should drive the motorcycle and asked him to take a breathalyzer test. George's friend said, "Up yours" and took off on the cycle.

The policeman jumped in his car and drove off after him. George saw them fade away all the way down Route 202 west until he couldn't see the tail lights anymore. It was completely dark, deserted of people, and George started walking slowly west on Route 202 to head home. It was quite a distance to his place. There were no cars moving in any direction, so he kept walking.

Suddenly, by a large deep cornfield, he heard a strange noise that could have been voices. He went a few paces into the cornfield, thinking maybe somebody had a phone that he could use or maybe someone soon would be driving in his direction. As he got closer, there were people, but they were dancing around a fire singing some pagan-like ritual song. He couldn't get out of there fast enough—obviously they were some witches coven. He started running on Route 202 until he became tired and stopped.

Finally, he saw a car coming his way and put out his thumb for a ride. It was a huge, old, pink Cadillac convertible driven by a silver-haired gentleman who stopped and let him in. George told him, "I need to get to Street Road, so I'll go as far as you're going."

The driver had other things in mind. He wanted to take George home with him to get to know him better. At this point, if George was any farther against the passenger door, he would've been outside the car. The silver-haired gentleman realized he was getting nowhere and got a bit testy. He made George get out of the car. George jumped out and saw a payphone in the distance (there were few cell phones at this time). He called his buddy whom he knew would be awake, to come get him. Before his friend could ask him, "What happened?"

George blurted out, "Don't ask."

And the guy with his motorcycle? He unfortunately slammed his bike into a ravine where it was totaled. The New Hope cops threw the book at him. He was in jail a few days, lost his license, paid a huge fine, and had to go to classes for drunk drivers.

A 1978 pink Cadillac Coupe Deville is worth $8,000.

When I was managing the Chess King clothing store, there was a somber story relating to George Evanick. George started dating one of my employees, a sweet pretty girl named Donna. It got very serious and he felt like she was "the one." The feeling was mutual. I was very happy for them. Whenever I would close the store with any of my crew, the last words from me as we walked out of the store together was always, "Be careful driving home!"

One Saturday night after closing the store with Donna, we were walking out of the mall to our cars. I forgot to say it, but Donna said to me, "Hey, be careful driving home!"

We had a store meeting at 10:00 a.m. the next morning right before we opened at 11:00 a.m. for Sunday business. I arrived at the store and my assistant manager was already there as were most of the employees, and everybody was crying.

"What happened?" I asked.

My assistant manager cried out, "Donna was killed last night in an automobile accident."

It didn't register for me and I said, "Repeat what you just said."

He told me again, and I dropped to my knees saying, "I was with her just last night. How the hell did it happen?"

"She was driving a friend's convertible at a fast speed. The car flipped over, she was thrown out, and the car landed on top of her, killing her."

Everyone was hysterical. I hugged everybody and knew I needed to call George. When I tried, there was no answer.

Late that evening while I was home, George called me, and as I expected, he was an emotional wreck. To a degree, we all were. He'd heard the news from her family. There was nothing I could say to him. She was so young and had her whole life ahead of her. George felt she was the girl he was going to marry. I let him talk and talk to get the anger and pain out of his system.

A few days later, all our store employees went to the funeral as a group. We closed the store during open hours. I cleared it with my district manager, who was very understanding. The mall didn't scold us for opening late that day either. They knew the story. Donna's last words to me— "Hey, be careful driving home," with that sweet smile—still affect me. I forgot to say those words to her on that Saturday night, but she said them to me. It all seemed like a bad horrific dream.

George Evanick is a good guy who went through some trying times. He likes to remind me of the evening I left work very ill. I think I had a fever while working on my feet all day during the holidays. We met outside Oxford Valley Mall at a local bar/restaurant for a drink. I ordered a brandy on the rocks, which of course is unheard of. I wanted something strong to rid me of my sore throat and cold. George yelled at me, "I don't know you. Who orders a cold brandy?"

My body just wanted to die. I went home and crashed.

A pair of vintage Waterford Lismore brandy snifters, 5½ inches in height, are worth $50.

I started at Chess King while still in college. I worked part time until graduation when I was eventually promoted to manager, but I was still looking for a better job. I had a good crew with Patty, Jeanine, Shelly, Donna, Mike, Jeff, Sean, Julie, Karen, Theresa, Maureen, Rob, and others. These employees, I felt, were better than most at other stores. The staff would change as employees periodically went away to college or found a permanent full-time job.

With so many years in retail, I could tell when a person walked into my store if they were going to buy, just look, or steal. I incorporated a theft deterrent system where we split the store in five segments. If a person looked like a thief, the employee would alert the others on duty by saying, "Jake comes in at two o'clock tomorrow"—meaning a suspect was in section two of the store. This method worked both ways because it also inspired employees to be more alert.

A pair of 1980s women's Jordache dark blue denim jeans are worth $60.

It was difficult to find good employees for a part-time position in sales because I looked for smart, attractive people who knew how to dress themselves. This was not easy.

I employed a beautiful, intelligent girl named Maureen who was an outstanding employee. She worked for me for many months and excelled in all her responsibilities. This straight-A student could have been a model. Acting very despondent, she disclosed to me one evening that her boyfriend had broken up with her. I said she had her whole life ahead of her and she would probably meet some great guy in college who is handsome and smart like she was.

Instead, she said, "What about you?"

My mind raced, and in four seconds, I thought of all of the following: "She's nineteen, I'm twenty-four but I'm her boss. I'm such a boy scout trying to do the right thing here. But she's gorgeous and I like her. I can't take advantage, it won't look good with the troops, yet I know other managers do this ALL the time. Damn it."

I said, "Maureen, you are so beautiful and intelligent. You have it all, but I can't. You'll probably have a new guy by the end of the week. Please don't be mad. Let's forget we even talked about this. It goes no further and no one will know."

I think she may have been embarrassed. We walked out to our cars after work; I yelled over to her, "Be careful driving home," but got no response back.

She never came to work again.

When my assistant called her at home, her mother said, "She quit."

I never ever saw her again. She was the kind of girl you take home to meet mom. Then mom would love her and probably make plans for a bridal shower. These are some of the trials of being a retail manager in the 1980s.

A pair of 1980s Ray-Ban AmberMatic Aviator Sunglasses is worth $75.

In retail during the holiday season, it's nearly impossible to take off from work because of being sick unless you're in the hospital. You work late hours, especially during the holidays. I missed going to my friend Steve Stratton's wedding and some family commitments, all because of working retail hours. My mother hated it when I was late for Christmas Eve dinner when she made "the feast of the seven fishes" for quite a few people. This feast is a big Italian Catholic tradition; the main course and side dishes include seven different kinds of fish or other seafood. My least favorite of these is baccala, which is dried cod fish—yikes! The tradition represented abstaining from meat until the feast of Christmas day itself when we enjoyed a big beef roast or ham.

A nineteenth-century English Staffordshire Blue Willow large serving platter is worth $350.

Retail hours during the holidays are always killer. Very often you needed to work an "iron" day during this season, which meant working open to close. This was another good reason to get out of retail.

A vintage Evergleam six-foot aluminum Christmas tree in box is worth $200.

The district manager of Chess King was fond of me because our store was always in the top three out of twelve stores in sales each month, and our store shrink rate was always low. The shrink rate is the percent of merchandise missing since the last inventory. Therefore, we prevented theft very well. I liked our district manager as well because we had good communication and a respectful relationship. Then out of the blue, she was being pushed out of her job by the regional manager. I discovered soon it was because the new lowlife manager of the Cherry Hill, New Jersey, store had slept with our regional manager and then became promoted to district manager. It was like an ugly pulp fiction novel. Then my hardworking friends who managed other stores in our district were quitting or getting squeezed out because the new district manager didn't like that they were close to the old district manager. I was next to get pushed out by this harlot.

I knew I could get another retail job in a heartbeat, which I did, managing a Webster Menswear clothing store. I worked at Webster for about a year. I took some of my employees with me from Chess King, while the rest of my former employees quit working at my old store.

Before I left, I contacted the home office of Chess King in New York to make sure I received my two weeks of vacation pay before my last day, which they mailed to me in time. I found out later the new district manager was furious because she was hoping to discover a way that I didn't receive that compensation. Including my college days working part-time, I spent seven years at Chess King meeting some lifelong friends only to be driven out by a slimy, immoral, ignorant reptile.

A six-pack "Barrel O Slime" by Alibaba Inc. is worth $7, not a penny more.

CHAPTER 4

Gallup & Robinson

In 1987, out of retail, I landed at Gallup & Robinson in Princeton, New Jersey, an advertising and marketing research firm. It was a job that offered some fun with some great coworkers and a few slightly strange people.

Whenever someone would tell a joke in front of the quirky company controller, she acted very robotic and responded every time with, "Is that funny ha-ha or funny queer?"

The woman never laughed and rarely smiled. Comedian Robin Williams couldn't make this woman laugh—a very odd bird.

Robin Williams once said, "I went to rehab for alcoholism in wine country, just to keep my options open."

I've always felt people who are humorless get upset over everything. They wind up starting wars, big ones if they can and small ones if they can't.

A signed Robin Williams "Mork" 16-inch x 20-inch poster is worth $300.

My coworker Tom could make me laugh at any given moment. When I returned from a vacation, he had placed police caution tape around my office entrance. Another time, he glued a small photo of our company president to the side of a milk carton over the picture of a lost child with the words "Do you know me?" and the company phone number underneath.

A vintage Bowman Dairy milk crate, circa 1950, is worth $125.

It was a respectable working environment. Our department, Response Analysis, was supervised by the even-keeled Rich Zane. The hard-working staff consisted of Tom, Delores, Greg, Joe, Bruce, and me. Our job analyzing marketing and advertising research was fascinating. We profiled the sample of people in each print ad or television commercial for our clients. Profiling is based on a person's behavioral characteristics as well as their demographics. I learned a great deal about profiling people.

For example, middle-aged regular beer drinkers (who drink five or more beers per week) usually are from middle- to lower-class household incomes, play the lottery often, usually don't drink hard liquor, and remember Vietnam as a not-so-distant memory—your typical Budweiser drinker.

Today, a millennial beer drinker (ages twenty-one to thirty-nine, who drinks five or more beers per week) usually likes more expensive craft beers with their food, admires local beer companies they can adopt and call their own, and drinks slightly expensive beer but thinks of it as an affordable luxury as they pay off their college debt. They usually refuse to drink Budweiser, the beer of their parents and grandparents.

Advertisers would give their right arm to know exactly how their target customers live.

A Budweiser bowtie-shaped electric guitar by Fender with case, circa 1980, is worth $300.

Our office was located in a brick, three-story building on Harrison Street, several blocks off busy Nassau Street in Princeton; it also had a huge basement. This park-like area in Princeton hid a mix of businesses and some extraordinary houses. If you didn't have a reason to go to this office, you would never have known it was there because of the abundance of foliage.

A 1928 Princeton University yearbook is worth $48.

A vintage Princeton University pennant pin is worth $30.

For some reason, the Princeton area is a hub for advertising and marketing research companies. Many employees jump from one firm to the next for a better salary or position.

I liked G&R, as employees would call it. We had some household-name clients like Nestle Corporation, Panasonic, Hertz Rental Cars, Coca-Cola Corporation, Toyota Motors USA, the Campbell Soup Company, Ford Motor Company, and the Kitchen Aid Corporation, to name a few. We analyzed their print ads, television commercials, or radio commercials with due diligence. It was like giving the advertising firm hired by our client a report card. Therefore, advertising agencies usually didn't like us.

A 1920s Nestle's Hot Chocolate tin can is worth $50.

My title as a research associate was directly under the account representative in our company who personally dealt directly with the client. I had to make sure every client report and ad analysis were completely examined, edited, and proofed before mailing the hard copy out. This was before email and the internet.

When we visited clients with our reports, the ad agency people were included in the meeting. You always knew who the ad agency guys were because they wore ponytails, had shaggy hair, or had affected speech like Jack Kerouac, in contrast to our clients in their Brooks Brothers suits. Many of the client offices we visited were outstanding state-of-the-art buildings with incredible architecture and lobbies.

Our company research director, Bill Green, was an amiable guy with peculiar sayings from his native Midwestern upbringing. For example, if the percentage of the research was so small that it had no significant value to the report, he would say, "It's a nit on a gnat's nut."

It took a while to define all his expressions.

You needed to be careful if you asked Bill a question and didn't allow enough time to hear the answer. Otherwise, you might get caught in his vortex and remain stuck for half an hour or longer with no chance to leave his office unless you were dying or someone yelled fire.

"Made out like tall dogs"—no one to this day really knows what this expression meant. Some people thought they had a handle on it, but we could not agree; however, all agreed Bill Green was a smart, great guy.

A pair of Art Nouveau cast iron dog bookends, circa 1905, is worth $100.

There were many account managers to cover all the clients. A very colorful vice president/account manager was in a meeting that I attended. She was discussing how to keep clients. She was well endowed and said, "Sometimes you need to show the client your tits!"

She did not mean it as a metaphor.

One day soon after June 17, 1994, when O.J. Simpson was being chased by police in his Ford Bronco, our office received a call from a very intelligent woman who was vice president and director of advertising for Hertz Rental Cars. I had spoken with her once before. O.J. Simpson was the long-time spokesperson for Hertz for many years. He was practically married to Hertz.

My account manager was a veteran employee, but he was out on the road, so the call passed down to me.

She said, "Well, this isn't good for us." Long pause. Then she asked me, "What do you think we should do?"

Without missing a beat, I told her, "Take down any and all commercial and print advertising with O.J. in it. Have no comment to the press, not even the words, 'No Comment'—just silence."

And that's exactly what the company did until much later.

My account manager returned and had a message from Hertz that he wanted to share with me. It was, "Thank you." He smiled and said, "When did you start making policy for Hertz?"

One interesting side note: O.J. didn't own his white Ford Bronco; it was a Hertz rental.

An O.J. Simpson signed rookie Buffalo Bills football card is still worth $250!

While working at Gallup & Robinson, I started Imagine Antiques (the "imagine" portion of the title was a nod to John Lennon) and began exhibiting at shows throughout the Delaware Valley on a part-time basis. This was 1988.

My first shows were the Yardley Antiques show, the Cheltenham High School show in Philadelphia, and the Corpus Christi School show in

Montgomery County. All enjoyable quality shows, but sadly, like a sign of the times, most of these shows no longer exist.

An 1882 $10 Brown Back Yardley National Bank, Yardley, Pennsylvania, paper currency is worth $1,000. Note: the back of the currency is mostly brown as printed by the bank that issued these.

CHAPTER 5

How I Met My Wife

While working at Gallup & Robinson, I met some very pleasant people that I remain friends with today. My office was on the second floor of a three-story building.

It was 1988 when I spotted those long legs in a skirt walk by the open doorway to my office. Who was this woman I had never met before? Apparently, the controller for the company was replacing the accounting person for our office. We were introduced as the controller escorted new employee, Karen Willis, to meet all the troops at the company.

I was smitten and had to talk to this person, but the angel on my right shoulder said to me, "Don't do it. Don't date someone where you work because if it doesn't work out, you have to work alongside her and see her five days a week."

But the devil on the left shoulder said to me, "What are you waiting for? Did you see those legs? I don't know you anymore, you wuss!"

I wish I could say that my brain debated this for a long time, but it didn't. I overheard a conversation in the office that she liked Rod

Stewart. I listen to a lot of different kinds of rock music and other music like jazz and new age, but Rod Stewart was never on my radar; however, Karen was.

Learning that Rod was appearing at the old Spectrum in Philadelphia brought back so many memories of concerts I've seen there like Tom Petty, U2, Styx, Aerosmith, Cheap Trick, and others. I tried to get tickets over the phone, but Rod Stewart was sold out. I called one of those so-called legal ticket services named John's Ticket Service, and they had plenty of tickets for the show. To say they were expensive, well, the price of the tickets should have had us sitting on the stage being able to touch the snare drum, but I purchased a pair of tickets anyway. At this point, I had not asked Karen out for the concert nor did I know her answer—just to show you how ridiculously cocky I was.

Something about Karen was special, and I couldn't put my finger on it. I liked the way she carried herself and spoke. Knowing the tickets were on the way, I quietly went down to her office. I knocked on her door and walked in. Without a smile she said, "What do you want?"

Papers were everywhere, and I could see she had a lot of work to do. I said slowly in my most sincere voice, "Would you like to go to the Rod Stewart concert with me in a couple months?"

She beamed and pressed her hands forward on her desk and said, "Yes."

I responded casually with, "OK, see you later" and left, my heart beating like a kick drum inside my chest.

With two months until the concert, I asked her to lunch. We did this more often and actually got to know each other. Once we went to dinner at a restaurant near where she lived and also previously worked. Our server felt compelled to inform me, "Karen is really nice and down to earth."

I said, "Yes, I know."

Karen and I talked and talked some more, everywhere we went. It was so much fun just being with her.

We started officially dating when one of the vice presidents from our office saw us walking together outside on the streets of Princeton and we were holding hands. Inside the office, we never showed affection, only business.

I met her parents about a month later. Jim and Betty were originally from the South and had distinct southern accents. Karen was born and raised in New Jersey after her parents moved there. She didn't seem anything like them in any way and didn't have the slightest accent either.

Karen put herself through Rider College going to night school while working full-time during the day. She had a little help from the Charlotte W. Newcomb Foundation Scholarship that she earned, but she paid the rest of her tuition herself with no help from her parents. Her father finished high school, and her mother never went past the ninth grade. They both had to work at a young age to support their large families where they grew up, respectively, in Tennessee and West Virginia.

A Rider College sterling silver student council pin, circa 1958, is worth $10.

Karen wasn't just someone I admired for her beauty and intelligence, but I also admired her initiative to go to college and get a degree and her drive to achieve success in the world—all without the assistance of her parents.

I was also in awe of this woman who persevered and survived the poisonous atmosphere of an active alcoholic environment with her parents, which bordered on the abusive. One such story involved Karen's little terrier dog.

One evening, Karen came home from work very late to learn that her father, in a drunken state, had accidentally left the side door open. Karen's tiny terrier scooted out of the house and onto a usually quiet street. The little pet was run over by a hit-and-run driver. When Karen learned about it and confronted her father, he snapped, "I never liked that dog anyway."

There were many other stories that only reinforce my belief in her ability to overcome adversity and misfortune at home. Karen conquered all of these hardships. Her parents both died young due to alcoholism. Karen is truly a role model for people in Al-Anon, an organization for people who live with alcoholics.

The more time Karen and I spent together going to clubs, museums, flea markets, the theater, movies, restaurants, and the shore, and the more time we spent just talking, the more I realized she was "the one"—the one I wished to have by my side for the rest of my life.

When we finally went to the Rod Stewart concert, I actually enjoyed it. Rod, who loves soccer, started off the concert by gently kicking soccer balls into the audience.

A Rod Stewart autographed soccer ball is worth about $400.

On a chilly day between Christmas and New Year's in 1988, Karen and I went to St. Patrick's Cathedral in New York. The church and the rest of New York were all dressed up for Christmas. The cathedral had life-size statues in a large manger near the main altar including real livestock and hay all over the floor. St. Patrick's Cathedral never looked more festive with crowds of people everywhere. The large stained-glass windows are magnificent.

Early church stained glass that is 6 feet by 7 feet in size is worth around $4,000 depending on its ornateness.

I had broken off two engagements in the past that I knew didn't feel right or fair to either party. With no ring on me in the middle of St. Patrick's Cathedral, it seemed like the right time. As we were about to leave, I turned to Karen with my heart pounding and asked her to marry me. She beamed, hugged me, held my hand, and made me race outside across the street to Rockefeller Center to watch the ice skaters. Then still beaming, she said, "Yes."

A pair of 1820 wooden ice skates in excellent condition are worth $185.

In early 1989, we moved into a small apartment together. We were married in a tiny, perfect little 1810 church called St. Philip's Chapel in New Hope on March 31, 1990. The church holds about fifty people, and that's how many guests we had for our quaint wedding, which we happily paid for ourselves. We paid ourselves because my parents insisted we invite the world to our wedding—the guy who delivers the morning paper, the barber who cuts my father's hair, the cashier who rung up my mother's purchase at Macy's, the guy who pumps the gas, and so on—you get the picture. Karen and I wanted a small wedding.

Therefore, we had close friends, our uncles and aunts, close people we worked with, and our parents. That's it. Our reception was held at the now Bowman's Tavern on River Road just south of New Hope. It was perfect, exactly what we wanted, and everyone had a good time.

After the reception, we flew to Disney World that night. We had a magical week with Mickey and company. It was Karen's first visit there and such a great escape. When we returned the following Saturday, my parents had a post-wedding party at their home in Holland, Pennsylvania, with more than eighty people.

A 1960 Mickey Mouse bobblehead nodder, made in Japan, is worth $40.

My parents treated Karen more like a daughter than daughter-in-law. Karen loved them back and their lovely home. It was a close, warm relationship.

Our tiny apartment at Middletown Trace in Langhorne, Pennsylvania, was only three small rooms, but we made the best of it. We stayed there for one year. We had saved enough to get our first home in Newtown, Pennsylvania. We couldn't wait!

We moved into a townhouse in Newtown in 1993. After our two children were born, in 2002, we elected to stay in the same neighborhood but moved into a large four-bedroom single house, with the idea that maybe my parents might move in with us someday.

Some areas of the house required work, and the original 1990 roof needed replacement. We hired WG Siding, a great bunch of guys from Poland. On the last day of work, the supervisor, Gregory, gave me a few pounds of real Polish kielbasa imported from Poland. When Karen cooked it, the entire house stank for days. It needed to be fumigated, but Gregory's heart was in the right place. I would use them again for siding, roofing, or windows, but not the kielbasa.

A World War II Polish Army Merit badge in display case is worth $80.

The neighborhood was pleasant and safe. Our girls could ride their bikes in our cul-de-sac without much traffic. All the families were kind here. In particular, Bart Cerami and Matt Maher were the best neighbors anyone could want.

Yard sales in the spring were always fun, and almost all the neighbors participated. Bart and I arranged these yard sales for our neighborhood. It's amazing that when you advertise for a multifamily yard sale and the weather is good, you get tons of customers. We loved that house and our neighbors.

A vintage postcard of the "Brick Hotel" in Newtown, Pennsylvania, circa 1910, is worth $12.

CHAPTER 6

The Golden Nugget Flea Market

After Karen and I were married, we elected to get her Lasik eye surgery. When Karen was born, she had abysmal eyesight. As a child, her parents thought she was just clumsy. Karen started wearing eyeglasses by second grade and later wore contacts all the time. When I first saw her wearing eyeglasses, the lenses were so thick, you couldn't see her eyes. She was a perfect candidate for the surgery.

After her surgery, she looked at a wall clock and could read the time without eyeglasses. This event was paramount. Karen started to cry, and the nurses had to insist she stop because the tears were unhealthy for recovery. Her eyes had almost 20/20 vision, but later, she needed to get reading glasses like the ones in a drug store or a good flea market.

A pair of 1920s rimless 10K pince-nez eyeglasses with chain in original case is worth $130.

Of all the flea markets near me, my favorite is the Golden Nugget in Lambertville, New Jersey. You never know what you will find at a flea market. Many people bring items from auctions to sell.

At times when you participate at an auction, you may only want to bid on one item that appears on a tray lot. When there are not enough valuable individual items to bid on from one consignor, auction houses will load up a tray of items from that same consignor to get a respectable starting bid—hence, a tray lot.

If you're the winner of the tray lot, you have the item you want. But what about the rest of the pitiful stuff on the tray? You can give them away, or put them in the trash, or maybe bring them along with other unwanted items to sell at the flea market. It's a great place to unload things to people who may find them desirable. If these "unwanted" items sell, it's gravy!

A vintage Rosenthal china "Helena" pattern gravy boat with attached underplate is worth $15.

If you're selling at the market, you should take the time to thoroughly pack the night before and be able to rise early in the morning to get a table. Better yet, reserve in advance to make sure you have a table or tables. I often sold my parents' unwanted things at the flea market. Back then, it became a place where an antiques dealer may find something worthwhile. Now, it has also become a place where a dealer can unload unwanted stock that has been sitting for a while.

I feel uneasy when I bring some of the same merchandise to the same show one year later. You open yourself up to customers moaning, "So you still have those same Eagle bookends?" or whatever. It's almost embarrassing because then that customer starts to think there must be something wrong with the item. Or they say, "The price must be too high, because why is it still here?" This is how the flea market helps the dealer. It's good to unload some of these items at the market at least a year or so later.

Gold nuggets out of the American River, half a gram, in a vial are worth $24.

Sunday is the best day to sell at the flea market due to the larger amount of foot traffic; I have made money on Sundays just selling unwanted items at lowered prices. It's worth cleaning out your old inventory; plus, my wife likes to give me some unwanted household items to sell as well.

You may meet some unusual dealers here. One Sunday morning after I set up, the man next to me walked over. I had never met him before, but without introducing himself, he shouted out to me, "There's a lot of bees out today. I'm allergic to bees. If I get stung, go into my car glove compartment, get my EpiPen, and jam it into my thigh." And then he walked away.

Only at the Nugget do I see and hear some real offbeat people like this.

On another occasion in the early 1990s, I was selling under the roof pavilion at the Nugget. The car I drove at the time was a dependable Subaru Outback. I loved that car when driving through snow. It was great. A man I never met before, about mid-seventies in age, walked over to my tables where my Subaru Outback was parked behind my tables as usual. He said, "So, you're driving a Jap car!"

I presumed his father fought in World War II and he hated Japanese people or he was some union guy. I said to him, "My mother drives a Ford made in Canada. My father drives a Pontiac made in Mexico. My Subaru was assembled in Indiana. Which car is foreign?"

The guy just walked away muttering.

A pair of Japanese Meiji period (1860-1912) Cloisonne Thousand Butterfly vases, 24 inches in height, is worth $47,500.

There have been famous people shopping at the Golden Nugget. New

York is less than three hours away from Lambertville, New Jersey. Friends told me they saw Jack Nicholson and Meryl Streep here around the time they made the movie *Heartburn* together.

I met actress Terri Hatcher who at the time was in the television show *Lois & Clark* years before the show *Desperate Housewives*. She was gracious and signed autographs.

A signed Terri Hatcher 8-inch x 10-inch photo is worth $100.

Actress Bebe Neuwirth from the television shows *Frasier* and *Cheers* as well as Broadway was reserved but pleasant.

My favorite sighting was actress Marisa Tomei who wore a hoodie and tried to be unnoticed but gave me a big smile and "hello." Today, she plays Spiderman's Aunt May in the movies. Of course, I told her she was great in all her pictures. I may have been slobbering when I said it. She was stunning just wearing a hoody.

A Stan Lee autographed "Amazing Fantasy" #15 Spiderman Cover, 11-inch x 14-inch photo is worth $310.

Back in the 1990s, a manager at the Golden Nugget named Heidi was the best at keeping all the dealers calm and pacified. If two dealers next to each other erupted in an argument, Heidi would tell them simply, "Stop this or you will never be allowed to sell here again."

That prevented any more yelling between vendors. Years later, the owner, Heidi's grandfather, sold the market and Heidi stayed another year to help acclimate the new owners, but she was eventually gone. To this day, the veteran dealers at the Nugget, including me, miss her and her ability to keep the peace and everyone congenial at the market.

Thankfully, most people selling and buying at the Golden Nugget are very sociable. Before I was a Bucks County Antiques Dealer Association member, I sold there many times and still do on occasion. I met a very interesting, quirky guy at the Nugget who later became a good friend. His name was Ken Friedman.

CHAPTER 7

The Anatomy of a Flea Marketeer

I met Kenny Friedman at the Golden Nugget flea market back in the early 1990s. He was an eccentric, funny, knowledgeable, irreverent flea marketeer who had been in this business for more than thirty-five years.

Like most flea marketeers, Kenny would sell anything that he felt he could make a profit on, regardless of age or value. This included reproductions, which is a cardinal sin among reputable antiques dealers. If there is a market for it, Ken would sell it as long as it's legal. Kenny would sell antique artwork right next to recent baseball cards. Vintage watches, primitives, nineteenth-century porcelain, swords, old keys, cut glass, and old coins would be alongside new Boy Scout patches, Hess trucks, reference books, and playing cards. It was usually quite the ensemble of merchandise. Ken would sometimes set aside special items for particular people with identifying nicknames like Joe, the "lighter" guy; Ray, the "watch" man; the "Bird" guy; the "Rock" king; Mike, the "postcard" guy; Joe, the "jewelry" guy; and so on. When he would see these particular shoppers, there was usually a transaction, and they were often Kenny's best sales of the day. Ken was always on the hunt for these people, and they very much appreciated it. When Kenny's old noisy green van would pull up to his usual space at the market, there would be a flock of patrons ready to see what gems he may have brought with him. Many reputable antique dealers were friends with him because they found the inventory they wanted. One such dealer was the late Lynn Trusdell, a BCADA member who dealt in Native American antiques.

If a flea marketeer did not bring food or drink with them, they tended to eat at the local luncheonette connected to the market, which did not always have the best-quality food. For Ken, convenience always beat out healthy food. In addition to his poor dietary habits, he had a five-pack-a-day cigarette habit. Almost everyone he knew told him to quit. Although he was not a pillar of health, Ken was no different than most people who grew up in the 1950s and early 1960s when smoking was a part of life. My two young daughters always pleaded with Ken, "Please stop smoking!" The most he would do is not smoke in front of them. Ken never had children but doted on many of his friends' children. He really liked kids, at least well-behaved ones. He always remembered my daughters' birthdays and remembered them at Christmas. This was his way with all his friends, and there were many.

For more than ten years, I often set up next to Ken with items I was trying to sell quickly. He and I shared knowledge with each other about various kinds of merchandise. Ken attended Syracuse University as an English major and later lived in Paris during the late 1960s, so he was well read in art and literature. It was sort of a learning experience for both of us. We helped each other with sales and researching and would watch over each other's tables for security. Like any kind of retail environment, shoplifting did sometimes occur. There was a code Ken employed if he thought someone was a shoplifter. He would shout out, "Take care of your paying customers." This phrase sounded the alert as Ken nodded in the direction of the suspect. Once they left the area, Ken often uttered an expletive and hoped they never returned. Once on a very bustling morning with many patrons, someone stole a loose roll of "Morgan" silver dollars in front of him. He was upset with himself the rest of the day and later considered it to be part of the business when selling at a flea market. It is actually no different than working inside a store.

The stories were not always grim or about theft. Most were about the humor of humanity. One of my favorites at the Golden Nugget flea market happened during a crisp autumn morning. An elderly man walked toward Ken and asked him in a strong country twang, "How much for the hollers?"

Ken asked him to repeat himself several times because he couldn't understand what he meant, but the old man said it the same way over and over. Ken and I, at this point, were trying not to laugh. Kindly, Ken walked around his table toward the man and placed his arm around his shoulder and said, "I'm sorry, buddy. I just don't understand what you're saying. Can you point at it?"

The man placed his hand on the boxes of Hess trucks. The strange accented man was saying "haulers" as in trucks! Ken asked him if he was from way down South. The old man said, "Yes, Cherry Hill!" (*about thirty miles south in New Jersey*).

Tears ran down my cheeks because I laughed so hard.

A 1965 Hess toy gasoline tanker MIB (mint in box) is worth $300.

At flea markets, people tend to expect to get better prices than they could at any show. One cold morning, a customer looked at Ken's telescope for sale that was marked sixty dollars. He asked Ken, "Would you take ten dollars?"

Ken stared at the man for what seemed like several days and finally asked him, "Where are you from?"

The man was taken aback by the question and left without answering. If a customer is serious about purchasing an item, they shouldn't haggle with the dealer by starting at less than 20 percent of the asking price. The dealer will never bargain down. When the guy left, Ken had some new twists on expletives I had never heard before.

An antique United States Navy brass 39 inch long telescope with wood tripod is worth $190.

There is much physical work for the flea marketeer who sets up at several different markets per week in extremely cold or extremely hot weather. Ken fit into this category. He would sell at three different markets during the course of four or more days per week. Working in this kind of environment can take years off your life. In some cases, these flea marketeers need to work or they don't pay their bills. It is a tough life for some, and it's usually displayed in their weathered faces.

This hard life caught up with Ken when he suffered a massive heart attack in December 2009. He needed bypass surgery after years of chain-smoking and poor eating habits. No one was surprised, including Ken. Only 25 percent of his heart was functioning. After a month of therapy, he was able to get around but was no longer a fixture at the flea market. He sadly told me that he could "no longer be a player."

He continued to go to some local auctions and would buy items for special customers. Ken was never the same after his heart attack. I still spoke with him frequently. Usually we would playfully joust about who was the better team—my Phillies or his "great Mets," as he would refer to them.

On November 26, 2010, at age sixty-eight, Ken Friedman died from pancreatic cancer that he just learned he had only two weeks previously. Ken was a funny, irreverent, kind person with many friends who cared about him including his girlfriend, Brenda, and his brother, Mark.

If we were going to meet at some genuinely choice auction, Ken was always quick to respond, "I will be there with bells on!"

I miss my friend, and I believe the bells are ringing where he is now.

A vintage large ornate brass church bell, 21 pounds, 11 inches tall, is worth $150.

CHAPTER 8

Working at an Auction House

After Gallup & Robinson, I worked for the Robert H. Clinton Auction Company for about a year where I absorbed a great deal of knowledge about the auction business. I also learned that Bob Clinton and his staff are extremely honest. The whole crew knows their role and does it well. Some auction houses are very unprincipled and deceitful, but not this one.

There is much to learn when working an auction: cleaning out the house with specific merchandise, labeling the stock separate from other consignors, setting up the auction room or an on-site house for auction day, wiring computer setup for the stenographers, placing merchandise sold separately versus in a box lot, supervising the parking, and having enough security coverage.

We were running an on-site house auction in an old Victorian farmhouse in the north end of Doylestown, Pennsylvania. The buyer was a builder who eventually turned all the acres into a large housing development. We met the very pleasant family who inherited the property from their recently deceased grandfather. When the woman was a little girl, she often played in the house.

On a hot August Monday morning, Eric Kessler, Bob Clinton's brother Donnie, and I needed to move all the contents on the second and third floors down to the first floor. Eventually most of it would be sold outside the house and lined up in rows on Saturday, the day of auction.

It was very hot that day, but as Eric and I climbed the large, beautiful wood stairs of this gorgeous home, the temperature seemed to get cooler to downright cold on the third floor. You would expect the temperature to get hotter as you climbed to a higher floor, especially on this August day and with no air-conditioning in the house.

You also sensed that you weren't alone up there. Eric said he felt someone was behind him the whole time he was on the third floor, but when he turned around, he felt it moved along with him and therefore he saw no one. Ghosts? According to folklore, when there is a ghost in the room, the temperature gets cold.

Eric and I found some secret passages on the top floor where there should have been walls. We thought maybe the house had been used as part of the Underground Railroad because it went through Doylestown. Or maybe it was used to hide liquor in the 1930s during prohibition. We weren't sure.

A tintype photo of a pair of African American women, circa 1870, is worth $65.

Donnie hadn't arrived yet. Donnie Clinton is as strong and tough as they come. We would joke that he could probably move the Statue of Liberty with a large rubber band and hand truck. Eric told me Donnie was not fond of ghosts! When Donnie arrived, Eric told him what had been going on. Donnie just smiled and said, "OK."

Donnie climbed to the third floor, and once again, it had turned so cold you could almost see your breath.

When Bob arrived, I told him the third-floor story about being watched and the temperature change. It didn't register with him. Bob started giving orders about where boxes and tables should go.

On Friday night, the night before the auction, Eric drew the short straw and stayed overnight in the house for security. Earlier that year, items had been stolen the day before an on-site auction in Holland, Pennsylvania. Eric built a bunker using boxes for the auction. He stayed inside this nest on a sleeping bag and cradled his revolver for protection. He said, "If anything comes at me in the middle of the night, I'm shooting first in that direction."

On Saturday morning, Eric was fine, the auction ran successfully without a problem, and we started to pack up our auction speakers, microphone, chairs, and equipment. The young lady owner arrived and we asked her if anything "funny" ever happened in the house. She replied with a serious face, "As a matter of fact, the house has a ghost. It's my great-grandfather. After he died, when I was a little girl, I visited my grandparents here and my deceased great-grandfather would always play with me in the house."

The young woman seemed credible and told us this story rationally. I still don't believe in ghosts, but this occurrence was so bizarre. I have never experienced anything like it again.

A vintage Halloween postcard with ghosts, circa 1910, in excellent condition is worth $50.

I learned a great deal about the value of various merchandise from Bob, his parents, his brother, and his sister. I also discovered how an auction operates, especially an honest one. This was the mid-1990s.

———— ◆ ————

When I was a kid sick at home, my Grandmother Rose would visit and watch television with me. We would laugh, and it made me happy she was with me. She always knew how to make me feel better in any given situation.

In 1993, Rose was diagnosed with cervical cancer. After many rounds of chemotherapy, sadly, there was nothing more the doctors could do. I was alone with her at her Brigantine home, and I knew she was in some pain but stable.

I wanted her to watch a comedy on television. Although it wasn't her usual television fare, we watched a rerun of the *Fresh Prince of Bel Air*. It was the episode when Will Smith subtly overheard his young cousin, Ashley, who had just turned eighteen, discuss how she was planning to have sex for the first time. Will was not happy about it, and every time he saw her, he shrieked. My grandmother roared with laughter every time Will Smith cried out. It was a lively show, and we had a good time laughing together.

A Will Smith-signed Fresh Prince script called "Knowledge is Power" is worth $250.

Laughter absolutely helps forget the problems of the day. My grandmother passed away on September 23, 1993, a year and a half before our first daughter, Emma Rose, was born. Her middle name is a tribute to my grandmother.

CHAPTER 9

Art Directives

After the auction house, I worked for a couple mind-numbing companies that wasted my time although I did meet and keep some great friends including John Skalski and Lynn Chesna, both of whom I remain in touch with.

John also grew up in Philadelphia, so we had similar roots and the same sense of Philly humor. We always made each other laugh with random pop culture trivia. John would say to me, "Leadbottom is on the way." "Leadbottom" was the nickname for despicable Captain Binghamton from *McHale's Navy*. Other references were the evil "Dr. Loveless" from *The Wild Wild West*, "the Penguin" from *Batman*, and of course "Danger Will Robinson" from *Lost in Space*.

I fondly remember those television shows. By sharing humor, John helped me keep it together when we worked for some very perplexing and depraved people.

A 1965 Revell model for McHale's Navy *P.T. 73 torpedo boat with original box, including four original figurines, is worth $140.*

Lynn Chesna was my administrative assistant at one company. She and her husband, Eric, and I became fast friends. We had similar tastes in music, antiques, flea markets, movies, and humor. Lynn played keyboards and sang in a band years earlier. We have a common bond with popular 1980s music.

Some years ago, Eric Chesna drove from their home in Upper Darby, Pennsylvania, to see me at the old Sovereign Bank Arena Antiques Show in Trenton. He knew I would be exhibiting alone and thought he could assist me and he was interested in shopping the large venue. He worked for an ad agency in Philadelphia where one of his coworkers happened to be a real jerk to other employees. This coworker stole lunches from the company refrigerator and was nasty at meetings.

Eric, who frequented flea markets all the time, found a large photo of a truly ugly family dressed exceptionally well. He fit the photo in an ornate frame and secretly placed it in the jerk's office, mixed in with his other family photos. Eric never told him or anyone at the office what he did. Maybe the coworker got the subtle message that he's not such a fine employee. Later on, the jackass sheepishly became a slightly better person in the office.

Eric was a super great guy who was loved by many people and always helped others, including me. Years later, Eric succumbed to cancer at a young age. It was a great loss and it crushed Lynn.

A late nineteenth-century Eastlake walnut gilt frame, 11 inches by 12⅞ inches, is worth $60.

Eventually in 1999, I worked for Rochelle Eisenberg who owned Art Directives when it was located in Fort Washington, Pennsylvania. Art Directives involved the interesting business of appraisals on antiques and personal property. Working here gave me access to some of the most beautiful homes surrounding Philadelphia, and I met some high profile and curiously eccentric people. I learned that in the appraisal world, discretion is most important. Client names are never divulged. I also was educated from some of my colleagues about furniture, textiles, art, ceramics, and the ridiculous prices that designers pay for new art glass.

Replacement value appraisal is defined as: The highest price in terms of cash or other precisely revealed terms that would be required to replace property with another of similar age, quality, origin, appearance, provenance, and condition, within a reasonable length of time in an appropriate market. This is the same as retail value.

Fair Market value appraisal is defined as: The price at which the property would change hands between a willing buyer and willing seller, neither being under any compulsion to buy or sell and both having reasonable knowledge of relevant facts. This appraisal is used for a charitable donation, a divorce, or an estate of a deceased person. It is similar to an auction value and tends to be about half of the Replacement value or retail value.

An interesting but my least favorite type of appraisal is a Fair Market value appraisal for a divorce. A court may deem it is necessary when dividing a property between a couple. What usually happens is the divorced husband and wife will argue over property that doesn't have much value. They simply don't want the other person to own it.

We once had a client who needed specific items appraised in the house of his soon-to-be ex-wife. The house was a beautiful split-level home in a housing development in Bucks County. My boss and I arrived to the house in separate cars and were told to wait until our client showed up. He arrived at the same time as a police unit with male and female police officers. We learned there was a court order and our client's proximity was prohibited to within one hundred yards of his wife unless the police were present. We left our two cars, while the young, beautiful, scantily dressed wife came outside and headed toward her husband. They both started screaming and cursing at each other on this sweltering 90-degree day in August. The police were nearby during this scream fest and a female officer approached me and said, "So, how long have you been doing appraisals?" as if this were business as usual for her.

As we entered the house with the wife, I noticed the air-conditioning wasn't on. It was hotter inside the split-level home than it was outside. After about fifteen minutes taking photographs and writing down descriptions as appraisers do, I needed to take my jacket and tie off. The heat was unbearable. If I'd unbuttoned my shirt anymore, I'd need a stripper pole. It made sense now that the wife was barely dressed and sweating due to the heat inside the home. My boss was looking a little dizzy and said to me, "I have to leave. Take over and finish." I couldn't blame her. She bailed, and our client left, followed by the police. The wife put on the air-conditioning while I was up in the 105-degree attic, sweating profusely and photographing a chest of drawers not worth fifty dollars. She found me and offered a tall glass of water, which I drank in seconds. She was so much more courteous after her husband left and asked me if I wanted another drink. I couldn't have said yes fast enough. I finished my work, thanked her for the water, jumped into my car, and put the air-conditioning on full blast. Apparently, the wife didn't want to make our job easy for us while her husband was there because he was our client. To me, the saddest part about a Fair Market value appraisal for a divorce is the pictures of the adorable little kids throughout the house. They didn't ask for this.

A 1940 lithograph of the play The Divorce Question *by Rowland & Gifford, 21 inches in height x 15 inches in width, is worth $125.*

My work at Art Directives was interesting and I was paid well, but the commute to our office in Fort Washington was wearing me out. It wasn't the distance but the constant traffic both ways. I was behind or in front of so many vehicle accidents on the Pennsylvania Turnpike during rush hour that statistically, I felt I was destined for a collision sooner or later. I lost count how many accidents I saw and was close to on the turnpike.

A 1940's Pennsylvania Turnpike badge and hatpin are worth $85.

Karen and I had two toddlers at this time, Emma and Julie. Rushing home to a family emergency could never be a rush. Our daughters had so many allergy health issues. It seemed like we were at the pediatrician's office or the allergist more often than at home. At the earliest, with traffic, I was lucky to get home in sixty minutes if I was speeding.

Besides Rochelle, I learned a great deal from another employee, Walter Ritchie, who graduated with a master's degree in decorative arts from Carnegie Mellon University. Brilliant in his descriptions of antiques, I took a night class at Temple University that Walter lectured. He had previously instructed decorative arts classes at George Washington University. He was a wealth of information that came in handy for future appraisals.

A signed copy of How to Win Friends and Influence People *by Dale Carnegie, dated 1939, is worth $495.*

I also learned a great deal about consistency and the proper way appraisal reports are completed from another coworker named Vicki Sullivan. There is a specific way appraisal reports need to be conformed according to Uniformed Standards of Professional Appraisal Practice (USPAP). It's important you proof your work for consistency. All reports were signed off by Rochelle.

Rochelle had been an appraiser for a very long time and had accumulated a volume of knowledge on varied types of antiques. She was also a good teacher. Years earlier, she assisted one of the appraisers on *Antiques Roadshow*. Most people don't realize that the appraisers on this program have a day or two to research the item they admire before they get taped for the show. Producers decide what to choose and what would be interesting for television. To cut costs today, Roadshow producers will make three episodes during a visit to one city at a time. It makes sense because the appraisers see hundreds of people who turn out for the occasion. *Antiques Roadshow* has been the number one Nielsen-rated show on PBS for more than fifteen years.

The highest appraised item on Antiques Roadshow *was a Patek Philippe pocket watch, which is worth $1.5 million today.*

Rochelle knew Leigh Keno, who with his brother, Leslie, usually talked about furniture on *Antiques Roadshow*. She had me confer with him through an email about an antique table. He responded right away and told me to give regards to Rochelle. He is a very down-to-earth guy. This email exchange was during my first month working there. I found it exciting that I could contact one of the best in the business to get a reliable and quick answer.

After a few years of completing appraisal courses, I became a certified personal property appraiser and changed my business name to Imagine Antiques & Appraisals.

Eventually, I left Art Directives in 2004 and started my own appraisal service while still selling at antiques shows. To me, Art Directives was like gaining additional years of college. I have many fond memories there. I learned so much about appraising from a great mentor in Rochelle Eisenberg. At one time, Rochelle told me, "With all the knowledge you're gaining, you should be paying me to work here."

Let's not get crazy.

Some of the items I've seen over the years included a William Merritt

Chase oil on canvas portrait of James Buchanan worth $160,000 and a nineteenth-century Regency mahogany secretary bookcase worth $3,000. Some furniture today is worth less than it was twenty years ago. For example, a nineteenth-century painted child's high chair is only worth $300 as opposed to $900 in the 1990s and a Victorian armchair with needlepoint seat is only worth $250 but previously would have been $800 in the 1990s.

CHAPTER 10

The BCADA Beginning

I knew of the Bucks County Antiques Dealers Association (BCADA) but never did I think I would want to become a member because some people I knew in this group were either arrogant or pompous. This describes the "old guard" in this club. Little did I realize how big a part of my life the BCADA would turn out to be.

Since 1966, this group has been rolling along in the antiques business while other similar groups withered and died. Some of these nearby groups that eventually vanished included the Montgomery County Antiques Dealers Association, the Delaware Valley Antiques Dealers Association, and the Pennsylvania Antiques Dealers Association.

Today, it's not hard to believe that these organizations don't exist anymore. There are fewer shows and antiques clubs because sadly, there are fewer antiques dealers.

In early 2005, unbeknownst to me, my long-time casual friend and dealer Mike Ivankovich had been pushing to get me into the BCADA. The president at that time, Endora Montgomery, believed that to be a member, you needed to be a dealer of primitives and country merchandise. It was not an actual rule, but it was understood you needed this type of stock. Mike himself didn't carry this stock, but his long resume in the business and the fact that he lived in Bucks County kept these "old guard" members from preventing Mike from getting into the BCADA when he joined.

There is nothing wrong with country and primitive merchandise. You need to have this genre in every or any antiques show, but in my opinion, you do not need it in the entire show unless you describe the show that way. For example, the long-running Elverson Antiques show runs this way, though it's actually a "high-country" show meaning only high-end country and primitive merchandise, expensive but high quality.

A nineteenth-century handcrafted three-legged wood milking stool with original paint is worth $180.

You also needed to be living in Bucks County to be a regular member at that time. If you weren't living in the county, you could not be a voting member but were labeled an associate member. At this time, the only reason to be an associate member was to be invited to exhibit at the annual show, which was located at Delaware Valley University on Thanksgiving weekend.

A pair of Turkey Candy Containers, circa 1900, unmarked German, 3¼ inches tall, is worth $50.

A turkey soup tureen, English Staffordshire, 11 inches in height, circa 1920, is worth about $225.

Mike Ivankovich pushed for me to join the club with the president. He told her, "We need some new younger blood because the club is getting too old as a group and Bill knows something about promoting and managing shows since he manages the Bucks County Antiques Show in New Hope."

From 2001 to 2011, I created and managed the Bucks County Antiques Show. I started this show because I believed many antiques show promoters weren't accomplishing their job properly and I felt I could do better.

It ran every second weekend of April at the Eagle Fire Hall in New Hope. The money at the gate went to the Elizabeth Glaser Pediatric AIDS Foundation. My wife and I very proudly donated over $30,000 to this great foundation over the years that the one-day show functioned. For our efforts, we were invited to attend a big gala event with other donors in New York but unfortunately could not be there.

We are fond of this charity because 89 percent of every dollar raised goes directly to programs that are reaching as many children and families as possible. This foundation earned the highest rating of four stars from Charity Navigator and an accreditation from the Better Business Bureau. At least today, if you have HIV, they can prolong your life with various medicinal cocktails including new experimental medicine that prevents a person from getting the disease.

By 2011, I was worn out after ten years of managing antiques shows and helped several other antiques shows behind the scenes. I was done with managing shows—or so I thought.

The BCADA voting process back in 2005 involved a member candidate filling out an application, the member chair visiting the prospect's merchandise at a store or show, and at the next meeting, a vote on whether or not to let the prospective member join.

Members Mike Ivankovich and his wife, Sue, ran the one-day BCADA outdoor summer show at the Moravian Tile Works in Doylestown in late June for four years. This show ran from 2002 to 2005. I exhibited at all four of these summer shows. The first year, I was set up next to the wonderful Brenda Farmer, a generous BCADA member who taught me a lot about paper and postcards. She was a very no-nonsense, intelligent lady who was not arrogant or pompous but sadly died a couple years later.

A 1909 postcard of "Perkasie, Bucks County on Fourth Street" in mint condition is worth $15.

During the first three years of the outdoor Moravian Tile Works Antiques Show, it rained, and during the last year of this show, 2005, it was 96 degrees. Mike was absurdly blamed by many of the exhibitors for the weather issues all four years. Mike said, "That's it. I'm done with this."

I couldn't blame him. He, his wife, Susan, and their team had done all the hard work to set up the show while most people didn't have a clue of what was involved. Running a show is a thankless job with a lot of behind-the-scenes work. You need stamina, good people, and a lot of free time to run any show.

Mike learned a lot about antiques by being an antiques dealer for many years and an auctioneer working at various auction houses including his own auction house. He specialized in Wallace Nutting prints from the early twentieth century. These prints also included all of the Nutting contemporaries like Davidson, Thompson, Sawyer, and other early photographers. Mike was also a good, certified generalist appraiser. He wrote books on Wallace Nutting, early twentieth-century hand-painted photography, and downsizing your Home, among other topics. He was also at one time president of the Pennsylvania Auctioneers Association. He owns a variety of websites that cover all these areas. He has a very well-rounded background. Mike is the kind of auctioneer you want if you need an auctioneer for any occasion.

A hand-colored photo of "Blossoms at the Bend," 16 inches x 20 inches, by Wallace Nutting is worth $100.

In the spring of 2005, Mike approached me at Alderfer's Auction about joining the club in a somewhat quiet corner while the auction was occurring. I asked, "Why me?"

Mike said, "We need new blood and the club is getting too old."

I filled out an application as was done back then and handed it directly to Mike as he requested. I wasn't that sure I wanted to join.

An antiques dealer friend of mine once told me a story about a BCADA member. This member visited the home of an elderly woman whose husband had just passed away. She needed to get rid of all her antique furniture because she was moving into an assisted living facility. The BCADA member gave her a low-ball price knowing she had no idea what all the furniture was worth. Then he made her sign a document stating that she couldn't change her mind. The woman later found out she was taken for a large loss due to her lack of knowledge. She was out hundreds of dollars. The dealer did not commit a crime but just lacked ethics. I'm not the guy who looks the other way. I don't condone or appreciate how this person took advantage of this senior lady. Not only did he show himself to be a villain, but he reduced the reputation of antiques dealers in general by his actions.

In addition, the Member Chair, Babs Hamilton, vetted my merchandise at the June 2005 Moravian Tile Works Show. Babs reminds me of the woman who played the witch in *Wizard of Oz* without the flying monkeys but with the same personality.

The Wonderful Wizard of Oz First Edition, dated 1900, signed by the author, Frank L. Baum, sold at Christie's auction for $152,500.

I waited four months, and finally, Mike called me in October to tell me I had been voted in as a member of the BCADA. I went to my first meeting in December 2005 at the beautiful and expensive Logan

Inn in New Hope, where they always held most meetings. The dinner was delicious. We dined while a piano player sang old show tunes and told stories.

There were other new members there too, including Mike and Judy Young of Young and Old Antiques. Mike and Judy are always fun to exhibit with at a show. The Youngs carry sterling silver items, crystal, glass, linens, and jewelry.

I recognized a few faces but barely knew anyone there among the twenty-five-plus people in attendance. Some of these members had trouble walking, talking, and breathing. I thought to myself, "Mike was right, the club is getting old."

A Cartier sterling silver cigarette box, wood-lined hollowware, circa 1930, is worth $1,400.

In the mid-1980s, the association had fifty-eight memberships. In 2005, it had twenty-four members and fourteen associate members (members who lived outside Bucks County). The club was slowly losing members each year. Adding new, quality members had to be a priority or the club would die.

CHAPTER 11

President Mike Ivankovich

In the beginning of January 2006, BCADA dues were handed in and many of the people from the December 2005 dinner meeting did not return as members. As per the bylaws, elections are held every June. I told Mike that he should run. He immediately told me NO. I pushed again and reminded him about the changes he could facilitate and how we could make the club more than just a simple "Country" Antiques Dealers Association; plus, it would look good on his already long resume.

He then said to me, "You run for president."

I said, "Too soon for me. These people don't know me yet. Think about it, especially since Montgomery wants to step down as president."

Three late nineteenth-century primitive wooden nesting pantry boxes with the largest at 9¾ inches in diameter, are worth $120.

It took a while, but Mike decided to run for president with the genial Mark DePorry as vice president. At his first meeting, Mike helped instate a new bylaw that said any member, no matter where they lived—outside Bucks County or not—would be a full-fledged member with all voting rights. Great idea!

Mike was president for two years. During the first year, Mike came to the meetings, we had some guest speakers, and it was fun. Having guest speakers on a semiregular meeting basis was a great idea!

Vice President Mark DePorry added a new feature: "The Newsletter," which featured a summary from every meeting in case you missed it. This newsletter included information about the guest or member speaker, important dates, new members, and any other important issues. It was a good vehicle for any member who couldn't make the meeting—another great idea!

A 1962 Objectivist Newsletter with cloth binding is worth $140.

Mark DePorry, a real gentleman, was an expert on fixing pottery as well as a dealer of pottery. He's retired now along with his very sweet wife, Sandy. Mark has serious back issues and can't sit too long or stand too long, but this couple always volunteered for admissions table duty at every BCADA show.

An early Victorian bench-fitting gem cutter is worth $300.

Mike, interestingly, cancelled what was to become our last show at Del Val College during the 2006 Thanksgiving weekend. This cancellation was a good idea. It was pointed out that we hired a firm to run the show for many years under Endora Montgomery as show chairperson. But we didn't make much money, and it became very hard to fill the show with exhibitors, possibly due to the high booth rent and smaller patronage each year. It seemed that all of a sudden, many dealers did not want to exhibit at this show. It was the right move by Mike but led to the consternation of some members.

The rent for the show was $450 to $600 for a booth, including walls, depending on the size of the space. This cost was outrageous in my opinion due to the amount of traffic at the show, which averaged

600 to 700 people. That same year, I exhibited at the Valley Forge Show run by Renninger's, which had booth rent at $450 and up, but there were well over two thousand patrons! Financially well worth it.

A 1910 Rowland & Marsellus "Valley Forge" souvenir plate is worth $40.

I suggested to Mike that we have a vote among members to not have walls in our show to bring down the rental cost. It would also give us two fewer days of show setup and breakdown. The walls cost us almost $6,000 to have in the show, which was more than the $5,000 rent at Del Val College for the weekend.

The "wall company" would setup the walls on Wednesday before Thanksgiving. Then Friday after Thanksgiving was exhibitor setup day, which added more expense with Del Val College because we rented the space on Wednesday, as well as Friday, Saturday, Sunday, and Monday morning (which was wall breakdown day). Without walls, we eliminated Wednesday and Monday rent to the school and eliminated wall expense, lowering the booth rent to maybe $300 per space.

Mike brought it up at the next meeting, we had a vote, and the majority still wanted walls. This result told me there were still too many older veteran members whose thinking was still in 1990. Back in the 1990s, antique shows would get thousands of patrons and dealers would always do thousands of dollars in sales. The "old guard" in this club needed to catch up with the twenty-first century.

The firm hired to run the show, as part of their agreement, were paid $2,000, yet they didn't take care of contracts. Endora did, which is a lion's share of the work. The firm took care of the setup of the show and the advertising, and positioned where dealers had their booths. The firm also had a free booth in the show (worth $450), received 10 percent of the gate both days, and received another $150 of discretionary money. This was idiotic—no wonder the club didn't make much money from the show.

Del Val College was also a problem because its football team had games on our show weekend, which would make parking incredibly difficult if any parking were available at all. One year, the school cafeteria ran out of food for our show because so much food was allotted for the football game crowd.

During Mike's second year as president, 2008, he was very busy personally with a multitude of jobs, lectures, his auction company, and appointments. He couldn't make it to every meeting. Mike decided he didn't want to be president anymore, and thankfully, Bill Perry, a wheelchair-bound paraplegic, of "Old Maps and Prints" stepped up to the plate.

An original 1830 Nathan Hale North America map, 5¾ inches x 3½ inches is worth $175.

While Mike was still president, I had recommended my friends, Steve and Eleanor Cheety of C & C Antiques as new members. They carried furniture, old tools, Limoges and other fine china, linens, and art. They are people of great character and principle. They have received accolades from many people who sold items to them saying they were treated with respect and paid fairly.

An antique knife sharpener Blacksmith grinder with foot pedal crank is worth $225.

When Babs Hamilton returned from seeing the Cheetys' booth at Brownsville Antique Centre in Trevose, Pennsylvania, she had nothing but unkind words to say at the next meeting.

In the Cheety's defense, I spoke up and said, "They run a spectrum of high-end to low-end merchandise in their co-op to make the rent. They never bring low-end merchandise to shows."

Babs didn't like them because she didn't know them. Mike spoke up and said, "We need new members and Bill is vouching for them. I say we vote them in."

And with that, the Cheety's had the majority of the vote. Some of the old guard may have gotten a little nervous.

An antique 9½-inch Hewing Broad Axe signed Spiller with wood handle is worth $150.

CHAPTER 12

President Bill Perry

Still show chair, Endora Montgomery, moved the show to Aldie Mansion in Doylestown during the month of March.

June 2008 election results were Bill Perry as president, Rollie Deacon as vice president, Judy Miller as secretary, and remaining officer, Bo Hamilton, husband of Babs, still as treasurer. Babs Hamilton was still member chair. Endora Montgomery remained show chair and pushed yet another BCADA show scheduled for March 2009 at Aldie Mansion.

After having both shows two years in a row at Aldie Mansion, the club took a financial bath and lost money both years. The mansion was beautiful, expensive to rent, but could only fit twenty-two dealers in the show. The stairway exhibitor was manned by my future buddy, Ashley King, a nonmember known as The Clock Trader.

A Federal mahogany tall case clock, bonnet with fretwork decoration and brass finials, cream-painted dial, signed by Aaron Miller, Boston, circa 1809, is worth $36,000.

For the Aldie Mansion show, Endora Montgomery as show chair was now taking $2,000 from each show, which ultimately put the club in the red both years! To be fair, Endora absolutely deserved some stipend to run the show. However, with such a small group of dealers, which equated less rent going to the club and only a fair gate, it was absolutely impossible for the club to make a profit at this venue.

A Show booth

Bill Perry knew he needed to do something and decided to make sweeping changes that upset many of the "old guard" and made some members quit the club at the end of the year.

First, he picked Vice President Rollie Deacon to be show chair. He had become a member one year before me and had no previous experience in managing shows. He was an expert on Civil War memorabilia.

A U.S. Civil War model 1840 cavalry sword with scabbard is worth $450.

Bill Perry had a flourishing business with his maps and prints. He usually sold well at shows. He loved talking to his customers about his products. The saying, "Hearing the story is worth the price of the item," fit Bill Perry very well.

An 1854 color map of the United States by W. Williams for Lippincott at 24½ inches x 29 inches is worth $800.

Bill anointed me as member chair, and with my support, he made Sue Ivankovich, Mike's wife, the webmaster to work on a new and better website, which would incur expense, but the club needed to make a statement in the twenty-first century—something better than the current stagnant website. It would give the club a website to cheer about with Sue's expertise. Her finished product was beautiful and easy to navigate. The club was going in the right direction.

A 1917 U.S. Navy copper compass navigator is worth $450.

CHAPTER 13

The New Member Chair

In February 2009, we were down to twenty-four members with all associate members now part of the regular membership. My first meeting as the new member chair was held at the Gardenville Hotel & Restaurant in Gardenville, Pennsylvania. We left the Logan Inn in New Hope because they would charge us $400 just for our room before we even arrived. And their desserts, though very delicious, were high-priced, typical for a restaurant in a tourist town.

Gardenville has excellent food thanks to Chef Jimmy, the help is sharp thanks to manager Kate, and our dining room is always clean. And it's more centrally located in Bucks County so that most of our members can get there for a meeting easily from every direction. The Gardenville Hotel dates back to the Revolutionary War days. Most importantly, the members like the food there and the free parking.

A 1781 State of Connecticut Revolutionary War soldier pay document is worth $120.

A rare 1910 Gardenville Hotel postcard in excellent condition sells for $20.

We sat in a circle of square tables with Bill Perry and Jan Allen, Rollie and Joan Deacon, Jean and Rich Rutter, the Youngs, myself, and a few others on one side and Endora Montgomery and some of her minions like the Hamiltons on the other. We would just argue all evening about the direction for the club. This happened meeting after meeting with no guest speakers and lots of yelling across the room. We were actually louder than the guys at the bar watching sports in the next room.

If I spoke up, Endora would try and talk over me, but the late Rich Rutter—God bless him—would shout out, "Let the young man talk!" Two things I liked about his outburst: Rich helped get people to hear my opinion, and I'm not that young. But by comparison to some of these people, I was a kid.

Rich was a large man with a big heart. He and his wife, Jean, were always kind to me.

Another person in my corner included long-time member Ginny Lovekin. Ginny carried great "Native American" artifacts. She would always say to me, "Keep doing what you're doing." Ginny was the sunshine chair for the club, which meant when someone was sick or a family member died, she would mail out a sympathy or "get well" card and sign it from the entire BCADA membership.

A rare 1920 to 1930 Navajo stamped coin silver and turquoise thunderbird eagle bird pin is worth $165.

I would state in a meeting, "There are many antiques dealers I know who would probably join our group if I ask them because they trust me. I think they would want to do our show and add something to our club. They know I wouldn't lie."

Endora Montgomery would counter with, "I know all the dealers, and there aren't any good ones left!"

I would state the opposite, and more chaos would ensue. At the end of a meeting one evening, Steve Cheety said to me, "I think I'm going to quit the club. This is no fun."

I told Steve, "Please just wait a little longer. It will get better, I promise. Trust me."

His response was, "I'm only here because of you."

When I became member chair, I suggested and then helped vote in Donna Panew, Jean Kulp of Jean's Books (also a good friend of Bill Perry's), Glen Cribbens, and Priscilla and Al Naylor, all in my first year. I chose antiques dealers who had quality merchandise and who I felt were sophisticated people.

A mid-century modern side table with brass corners by Tomlinson Sophisticate East, 16 inches in height, 22-inch square top, is worth $160.

Sometime after Donna Panew became a member, Bo Hamilton wanted to step down as treasurer. Bill Perry with my suggestion made Donna Panew run for and become the new treasurer in June 2009. The treasurer books and notes were in some disarray. However, Donna did a great job of organizing the club records. Endora and the Hamilton's left the Association after June elections which helped propel us to grow as a club.

As the new member chair, I was able to bring in the wonderful Erik Fleischer of Pineapple Antiques. Erik carries beautiful antique wood boxes and primitives. He wouldn't join our club as long as some old guard members were still there.

What some members may not appreciate or realize is that Endora Montgomery kept the club rolling along when it could have simply folded like other Associations. She also wanted to make sure any BCADA show looked good and she was an excellent primitives dealer.

An original paint Primitive Folk Art Firkin Bucket with handle, 14 inches high, is worth $130.

CHAPTER 14

Bill Perry's Second Year as President

Bill Perry and Jan always liked to discuss how well they sold, but so many genres of antiques were crashing in value. Pressed glass, American Cut glass, Depression glass, Staffordshire ceramics, Limoges China, American and European pottery, certain furniture, almost all collectibles, and other genres were all taking a beating.

A vintage pressed glass pedestal fluted fruit bowl is only worth $10.

A 9-inch pink Depression glass "Buttons & Bows" pattern bowl had devalued down to $8.

A Haviland Limoges hand-painted cream pitcher is worth $18.

An American Brilliant Cut glass 4-inch tall tumbler is worth only $8.

A nineteenth-century Staffordshire children's "B for Benevolence" mug is worth $10.

Because of this change, many of the old guard made up their mind to exit the club, saying, "It's not the same business anymore."

The fact is it's never the same and it's always changing. You need to change with the times, or you'll go broke sitting on unwanted merchandise.

During my second year as member chair, I helped bring in a lot of new faces. They included Ashley King of The Clock Trader; Lacey Brown, Elena and Hans Schmidt of Elena's Discoveries; Roberta Hollingshead; Benji Kidwell of Ivy Iris Antiques; Karen Taylor of KT Antiques; Doreen Dansky of Pentimento; Dan Worden of The Silver Solution; and Stanley Smullen.

To say I was busy working in the BCADA is an understatement, but I was very happy with more new members, less of the old guard, and moving in the right direction.

At the same time, unfortunately, Bill Perry's health was deteriorating slowly. He was in and out of the emergency room several instances that year with Jan by his side. New secretary, Judy Young, who knew Bill many years earlier when she was his nurse, told me he had nine lives.

Bill became a paraplegic in his early twenties after hitting a tree while skiing. He loved to ski. After his accident, his mother, a tough, strong woman, helped him start an antique map and prints business that became very lucrative with a big following of customers.

Bill Perry had courage and a big heart, was extremely honest, and would help anyone in distress. As a night owl, he would call me late at night and say, "Is it too late to talk?"

We would then talk until the morning about the future of the club and how to improve it. Then the conversation would take a turn because we had a mutual love of movies and pop culture. Our conversations sounded something like: "Who was the best Captain of the

A Show booth

Enterprise?", "*Psycho* was not Hitchcock's best movie!", and so on. He was always a lot of fun to talk to. He called me a real friend, and he knew I would do anything for him and vice-versa. For a guy who couldn't walk or stand, he stood taller than most people I knew.

An original Alfred Hitchcock 1947 The Paradine Case *movie script is worth $6,000.*

CHAPTER 15

The Glen Cribbens Story

In 2010, I mentioned to Bill Perry that member Glen Cribbens wanted to make some changes to our website. Glen's store contained a large array of mourning antiques and an assortment of brass birdcages throughout the place. However, there was something also seemingly sinister and spooky when you walked down the aisles. You would be surrounded by hair art that was the fashion in the Victorian age. People would use their late relative's hair for all kinds of framed art in the shape of wreaths or some type of flower arrangement. This art could include a photo of the deceased person or a picture of the town they were from. With many photos of dead people including babies in coffins or cradles throughout the shop, this spooky store was not for the squeamish. Young people into goth found the store entertaining. You would expect the *Addams Family* to greet you inside.

A nineteenth-century Victorian French framed palette hair work is worth $165.

A Victorian embroidered and fringe mourning skirt and blouse in mint condition is worth $220.

If you asked Glen what he sold, he bluntly would reply, "Dead guy stuff." There never seemed to be many customers in his store; however, he told me that he rented out his bird cages to movie sets, commercials, and photo shoots all the time, and it had been profitable for him. It all made sense because I knew the rent for his shop was very high.

A Victorian two-story Pagoda style wire and wood birdcage is worth $495.

A Victorian 45-inch tall wicker cottage-style birdcage is worth $250.

One windy day at his store, Glen boasted to me that he was having an affair with one of our BCADA members, Lacey Brown. Glen had helped shepherd her into the club. I liked Lacey. She's very knowledgeable in the business, very helpful at a meeting, and generally hospitable and gracious to everyone.

My wife's voice popped into my head saying, "Why does everyone tell you everything? What are you, Father Confessor?" She's right. This always happens to me everywhere I go.

I told Glen, "She has a husband and daughter; why does she do this?"

He said, "She's married to an accountant, and she's bored."

"How long?" I asked.

Glen replied, "A few years. She wants to move in with me but I won't because she has a daughter."

I'm supposed to feel Glen is noble in this gesture?

I sat on this information for a few months until Glen had the big idea that he wanted to make some changes on our website and wanted the codes from our webmaster to do it himself. He wanted to place some political ideas on the site but he knew we were a nonpolitical, nonsectarian club. He became very angry that he couldn't have his way, and therefore, he didn't come to another meeting.

Bill Perry learned his whole story, and with January approaching, he hoped he wouldn't renew his membership. Donna Panew, our treasurer, said she received her mail on the due date and Glen's dues weren't in it. The officers were happy.

Later that night, I received a frantic phone call around 10:00 p.m. from Donna. Yes, it seems I'm the guy who also gets the late phone calls.

Donna said she heard a noise like someone had opened her outer door. She went to the door, and between the screen door and front door was an envelope with Glen's dues in it. No one told him where she lived. Donna was frightened and very upset. It's kind of spooky anyone would deliver anything that late at night without telling the person in advance what their plan was. I told Donna, "Next time call the police. They're one minute from your home."

A vintage New York Metropolitan Police whistle with chain is worth $65.

I phoned Bill Perry about the incident, and he spent the night with girlfriend, Jan, drafting a letter explaining that the club would not accept Glen's dues because of his insistence on changing the website for political purposes. For a reason, it was a little weak, but it worked.

The letter was signed by all four officers—Bill Perry, Rollie Deacon (vice president), Donna Panew (treasurer), and Judy Young (secretary). It was mailed certified with his dues check included, and he was gone.

A 1956 Edward G. Robinson signed certified letter is worth $125.

I believed Bill Perry's real reason to not accept Glen's dues was more about the affair than anything else. And I told Bill (and I truly believe this), "It's none of our business what members do outside our meetings and outside our shows." But my words landed on deaf ears.

With Glen gone, Lacey called me and said unhappily, "Every time Glen and I join a club together, something happens and he's forced to leave and I have to follow him."

Lacey was aware that I knew about the affair. Was this a cry for help that she maybe disliked the relationship she was in?

Lacey stayed another year but left the club probably due to Glen's insistence. I can only surmise the bigger the club gets, the greater the possibility of crazy adult antics happening.

A few years later, I checked online to see if Glen's store was still there. To my surprise, there was a sign stating that the store was "closed due to the owner's health." It may have been more about lack of sales like so many antiques shops in New Hope.

Then while I was still online, I found something horrifying. Glen was on the sex offender list and had been convicted in 2001 in New York. The girl was only eight years old. I wanted to get sick. As member chair, it was more my fault than anyone that he was ever in the BCADA. I couldn't believe it.

Now I find myself checking every single person who is a prospective member to see if they have a police record.

A 1930 Prohibition-era Yolo County, California, Deputy Sheriff circle star police badge with double maker marks is worth $575.

CHAPTER 16

The March 2010
Vo-Tech School Show

Member Rollie Deacon was not experienced in running a show. As show chair, it was Rollie's job to contact members and nonmembers about exhibiting. With four months to go, I reminded Rollie to get started. He would reply, "I have plenty of time." I helped Rollie and Sue Ivankovich with wording the contract, and the contracts were mailed out to members who previously did a BCADA show. Of course, you can't always count on them to do a show year after year.

In February, Rollie exhibited at the Brandywine Antiques Show in Chadds Ford, Pennsylvania (home of the late artist Andrew Wyeth), where he expected to pick up some dealers for our BCADA show. The Brandywine Show is a long-running show, however, Rollie learned that Endora Montgomery was informing dealers not to do the BCADA show because it wouldn't be successful for them. BCADA President Bill Perry had his attorney mail a "cease and desist" letter to Endora, and this went away. Endora Montgomery was still resentful; I was consequently not surprised at all.

An Andrew Wyeth-signed limited edition giclee of Snow Hill, *unframed, is worth $10,000.*

Unfortunately, only fourteen members could exhibit at our show. Members gave many reasons for why they couldn't exhibit, including weddings, family commitments, health reasons, or other shows the same weekend. However, why would members exhibit at these other shows instead of ours? Where's the faithful dedication to the club? Member Benji Kidwell told me, "I'm doing the show because it's for our club." Apparently not enough members thought that way.

Member Roberta Hollingshead had recently learned that her son was coming home from Iraq the weekend of our show, but she said, "I'm committed to doing the show and I am doing the show!"

An Iraq Gulf War captured Iraqi Army bayonet with numbers is worth $250.

Then out of the blue, I received a call from Rollie late in the evening. He said, "I can't get anyone else to do the show; I need you to take over."

This call came with less than one month before the show! I was furious at Rollie as I thought about those many instances, he said to me, "Don't worry, I have plenty of time."

For the next few weeks, I was constantly on the phone trying to get quality dealers to exhibit. I was on the phone as late as 9:00 p.m. and then started making calls again in the morning at 9:00 a.m. I missed a few of my family commitments. It was an uphill battle because too many dealers kept saying to me, "Why did you call so late?", "I already have another show," "What's wrong with the show that you still need dealers?"

My wife said, "This is too much stress on you."

I was focused on doing a better job than the "old guard"; otherwise, if we failed with an inferior show, those members who left—especially the nasty "old guard"—could say, "These people have no clue what they are doing." I didn't want that negativity after all the positive changes made by presidents Mike Ivankovich and Bill Perry and with myself as the new member chair.

Bill Perry was upset with Rollie for dropping the ball. However, Bill was having lots of health issues and couldn't get that involved. Jan felt there was too much burden on him and felt he shouldn't be president anymore. Rollie planned to run for that office, but after the show debacle, I had some of my own ideas.

This show was the first BCADA show without walls, but exhibitors were allowed to bring their own and some did. One "old guard" member refused to do the show without walls. Even with the fewer dealers we had exhibiting, the show looked great and we didn't need divider walls!

On the day of setup, five of the so-called definite dealers Rollie achieved for the show never arrived. I called them, and they didn't care about missing the show because they had no deposit down.

First rule of thumb with any show: the promoter always receives at least a deposit from any dealer expected to exhibit at the show. Again, I was angry at Rollie.

Outside in the rain, in the soggy driveway during the middle of the Friday show setup, Rollie apologized to me about everything he didn't do. In fairness to Rollie, he was in over his head. The job of promoting a show may seem easy, but it's not. I should have seen it coming. In fact, it was my fault I didn't step in sooner to help.

We used three of my good friends as porters for the show. I picked

Wayne and Dave setting up the show

them because I knew they were dependable, would be on time, and would do a worthy job. They were Dave Callihan, Wayne Sia, and Mark Bindelglass. We still use Dave and Wayne today as porters. They know what they're doing.

Dave has helped me fix merchandise for sale like glass, furniture, and lamps. He has also helped me fix things in my house like our gas fireplace and lighting fixtures, and has helped me take old wallpaper off the walls. Not a fun job.

Wayne has also helped me with repairing things like our kitchen cabinets and helped paint our outside second-floor shutters.

Mark has been a good friend when I needed a sounding board. They are all great guys who also promote our BCADA show every year.

I met Mark many years earlier at a local auction. I was selling Girl Scout cookies with my daughters during the auction. Mark came over and said, "How much for the Thin Mints?"

I told him $3.50.

He bought a box, left, and then spun around back to me and said,

"Hey, Rain Man (like the movie), you gave me too much change."

And with that, we became fast friends with a mutual love of antiques and baseball. We went to a few Phillies–Mets games together. At Citizens Bank Park, with Mark wearing his Mets gear and me in my Phillies attire, we never argued and got along well unlike politicians today who could do much better.

A 1960s rare Mets bobblehead Nodder with blue shoes and white square base is worth $400.

I was only able to add ten more dealers to the show at this late date, giving us just twenty-four exhibitors in this large cafeteria. Dealers spread out if no one was next to them. For member Benji Kidwell of Ivy Iris Antiques, her booth seemed like the length of a football field after she spread out on both sides of her actual boundary. She went home and brought more stock to the show. Benji, a terrific sociable dealer, carries great primitives, advertising, and children's items.

A 1940s Jim Jak Cafeteria Coffee Dispenser, 4 feet in height, is worth $250.

Unfortunately, we had some exhibitors who were concerned about their location, as far as proximity to the entrance. I purposely took the farthest booth from the front door to prove the point that patrons will see everyone usually twice before they leave.

With any small show (i.e., less than fifty dealers), patrons will usually walk around the show twice to view everyone because the show is small and it wouldn't take much time to see all the exhibitors a second time.

The Vo-Tech School had plenty of room for almost any kind of show. The place was kept very clean and had no steps from the rear entrance to the cafeteria, where our event took place. However, the school charged us a lot of money including for tables and chairs that were already in the cafeteria! The chairs were two dollars each if used—just ridiculous.

A 1950s set of four kitchen chairs with red vinyl cushions and chrome legs is worth $165.

I felt like the school had taken advantage of our club. The old Heritage Conservancy Antiques show was also held at this location. You would think the school would be more open to reasonable fees. What else could go wrong? Regretful question, because it got worse.

At the start of the show on Saturday, we were hit with a hurricane and torrential downpours. There weren't any leaks in the ceiling, but the heat was off due to the weekend timer with the school, which they couldn't change. Dealers were freezing. Dealer Lorraine Wambold's lips were actually blue. Donna Panew needed to rush home because her large front-yard tree fell over and blocked her neighbor's driveway.

She never made it back to the show on Saturday, and someone had to watch over her booth.

In the foyer entrance to the show, the volunteer members including my wife, the Naylors, Jean Rutter, the DePorrys, and others had to paperweight everything everywhere on the table because the wind was so strong it would blow the papers down whenever the door would open with more patrons. The signs outside constantly needed to be placed back up.

A nineteenth-century rare blue Boston and Sandwich art glass paperweight is worth $295.

As far as the patrons who did attend, they consistently asked, "Where's the rest of the dealers?" With only twenty-four exhibitors, it was very noticeable in this large cafeteria.

We lost power off and on during the two days. When I would look for the elusive Fritz, our contact with the school's building and mainte-nance department, he was always missing. This guy became a running joke. When the lights came back on and there were no issues, he would suddenly appear. I was the one who needed to look for Fritz because our show chair, Rollie, had his ongoing health issues.

A 1925 Rhine-Westphalia Electric Power corporation 7 percent uncancelled $1,000 bond is worth $425.

With the terrible weather and the problems related to the show, we still had almost four hundred patrons. Some dealers did very well, while others underperformed. Even with the farthest booth from the door and being hardly in my booth as I fixed little problems, I still sold very well.

I felt the building, its costs, the ridiculous maintenance guy, and the whole vibe was awful and we needed to change locations. It's not advisable to keep changing the location of your show when you want your patronage to be able to find you easily each year.

My suggestion to President Bill Perry was to change to a venue that was less costly, move the show to New Hope because people know how to get there, change the date back to November, and change the show chair.

Bill Perry agreed.

CHAPTER 17

The Ballad of John and Nancy Scarpell

Around the time of the March 2010 show, after a long illness, member Nancy Scarpell died. She was the love of John's life.

John and Nancy were not only charter members of the BCADA since 1966, but they were also very proud members of the association. John actually included that fact in her obituary: "Proud member of the BCADA." Although they started with the club in the beginning, they were all for making the club grow into the twenty-first century, and they supported Bill Perry with any and all changes for the better.

In his younger days, John was a mail carrier; he also had a love for fixing country furniture. John had an amazing gift to restore and resell furniture back when furniture was selling well in the 1980s and 1990s.

A nineteenth-century North Carolina pine pie safe with double doors is worth $900.

John once mentioned that he didn't vote for me to become a member because he thought so highly of the association that no one is worthy to be in the membership. That's an interesting take on the club, though I don't necessarily agree with it. John is a sincerely good person who would give you any help you needed if you asked. He and Nancy specialized in country furniture, primitives, and Flow Blue china along with other smalls. John did not vote for me, but fast forward several years and John told me I was the best president the club ever had. Since he's seen all the presidents of this association since 1966, I was more than flattered.

A Flow Blue dinner plate by Charles Meigh, "Hong Kong" pattern, circa 1840, is worth $50 (in the 1990s, it was worth $175).

John and Nancy were married a long time. They loved hunting for antiques, loved coming to meetings, and loved all the other BCADA events when they felt up to it. They exhibited in all the shows, as well as in the summer shows that Mike Ivankovich ran for the club outside the Moravian Tile Works.

One of the sweetest ladies in the association, Nancy died at age eighty-five. John was beside himself. I called him periodically to see if he was OK. He did most of the talking. I think he just needed a sounding board.

He eventually took a lot of their merchandise and sent it to auction. The auction results were not kind. John made pennies on the dollar with such merchandise as Flow Blue china, kitchenware, Staffordshire, and some small furniture.

An 1870 Staffordshire model of a cottage, 8½ inches tall, is worth $200.

I'll never forget in 2002 something John said to me during one of my Bucks County Antiques shows that I ran in New Hope. After working many years in an advertising and marketing firm, I hate lying to the public about what they are going to see and hear. For one show

I promoted, we were expecting to have thirty exhibitors and one person couldn't do the show at the last minute. I was upset about it, but John Scarpell, who exhibited in my show, came over to me, put his arm around my shoulder, and said, "Do you think anybody is going to count?"

It hit me how simple and true his statement was. I laughed and said, "You're right. It's no big deal."

John made me feel better about the situation that I had no control over.

Of all the long-time members in the BCADA, they were two people who couldn't have been kinder to everyone, and they supported me with everything I did. Everyone missed and loved his beautiful Nancy. John was never the same.

A 19th century oil on canvas unsigned "Portrait of a beautiful woman" 30 inches in height by 25 inches in width, unframed, is worth $350.

CHAPTER 18

The New President

In June 2010, Bill Perry, in agreement with his girlfriend, decided to step down as president due to his health. Rollie Deacon wanted and expected to be president, but I had heard from other members that when he was president of the Montgomery County Antiques Dealers Association, he ran it into the ground. That group no longer exists.

With this knowledge and knowing how he was as show chairperson, I couldn't let Rollie get the BCADA president post and possibly hurt the club. I ran against him and won unanimously except for one vote—Rollie's. He was a little upset but congratulated me. Dan Worden was my vice president and Donna Panew stayed on as treasurer.

Dan Worden was wonderful as vice president because he always gave me objective guidance on any subject or problem within the association. Dan was previously the Upper Makefield head township supervisor in Bucks County for many years. Upper Makefield covers the area of New Hope and Washington Crossing, Pennsylvania. Dan was also in the United States Navy during the Vietnam War. He had more to do with adding the much-needed recent Veterans Cemetery in Washington Crossing than any other person. He fought against a large aggressive homebuilders corporation who tried cluster housing, contrary to the zoning law as a blackmail technique against the township. Dan is an honorable pillar who cannot be influenced by money or power. A deal was struck where both sides obtained the desired land needed, and thus, the Washington Crossing Veteran's Cemetery came into existence.

A vintage brass World War II Navy Submarine Veteran grave marker is worth $70.

I anointed Doreen Dansky as member chair and kept the wonderful Ginny Lovekin as sunshine chair. Doreen was perfect for the member chair role because she is an incredibly talented writer. Her reports were informative and thought provoking.

An Ernest Hemingway The Old Man and the Sea *1952 first edition with dust jacket is worth $400.*

New members from 2010 to 2011 with my shepherding included two great guys, Arthur Schwerdt and Larry Damato of August Farmhouse Antiques. The club added Eleanor Jenitis of ELtiques, Mark Milnes of Hidden River Antiques, Chris Wise of Errant Artifacts, and Dale and Sally Comisarow of The Painted Shutter. Also added was Ruth Peckmann of Antiques in Bloom whom I adore with her dry, wicked humor. By this point, we were up to thirty-six members.

Ruth Peckmann's business had started out decades earlier. She had a successful company called Andorra Gardens making wreaths and arrangements using dried flowers. Her wreaths and arrangements were wholesaled to Winterthur, Longwood Gardens, and elsewhere. While Ruth was in New York in the late 1960s, she saw Richard Burton and Elizabeth Taylor walking out of a building. Besides being gorgeous, Liz's eyes were actually violet. No wonder men were falling over themselves chasing after her.

A July 1950 issue of Movie Life *magazine with Liz Taylor on the cover is worth $100.*

The next show wasn't until November 2011. I found a place with potential or so I thought—a school not far from the heart of downtown New Hope.

Our meetings at the Gardenville Hotel usually included a guest speaker, and we had some great ones—Steve Cohen presented on local real-photo postcards of Bucks County, Claire Lavin discussed Halloween collectibles (in October of course), James Curran talked about period furniture, and Tom Rago discussed pottery. These meetings were a lot of fun.

A Delaware River, Bristol, Pennsylvania, real-photo postcard, circa 1910, is worth $25.

A 1940s papier mâché 6-inch-tall Halloween Jack O'Lantern is worth $40.

A nineteenth-century mahogany round-top wine table with three cabriole legs is worth $360.

A large pair of Art Deco Trenton Pottery Hexagonal aqua turquoise urn vases are worth $1,000.

———— ◆ ————

In 2011, my orthodontist had discovered I had a dead tooth that needed removal. No one seems to know why your teeth decide to die. It can just happen. I had chosen to get an implant with the help from a referred maxillofacial surgeon. Since the area was a difficult molar location, it was decided I would be placed under anesthesia during the procedure.

The surgery was successful except that I wouldn't wake from the anesthesia. They alerted my wife from the waiting room who proceeded to yell at me in the chair to wake up and I finally did. My wife always knows what to do.

A vintage dentist patient chair manufactured by Peerless Harvard, circa 1960, is worth $750.

CHAPTER 19

Bill Perry Dies

Three months before our November 2011 show, Bill Perry died on August 13. It wasn't unexpected, yet it still hit me because he was a dear friend. He didn't have a selfish bone in his body and was always looking to better the club. We both shared a favorite quote: "The needs of the many outweigh the needs of the few or the one."

At our September 21, 2011, meeting, I held a moment of silence for Bill. Then I told our members, "He wasn't just a fellow member to me; he was my friend and I will miss him."

With that, I almost wept because I thought about all the crap we went through—the scream fests at meetings with the "old guard," the two non-money-making shows at Aldie Mansion, the hurricane show—all of it just to get this club going in the right direction.

My wife Karen had to drive me home after the meeting. I was almost inconsolable because I thought about the other two friends I had lost recently, Chris Ducko (only age forty-nine) and Eric Chesna (only age thirty-three), along with Bill Perry (only age sixty-five). It all hit me at the same time—young and fairly young all gone. It was hard to accept.

Yet when I went to Bill's funeral the previous month, I was fine. Other members in attendance at the funeral were Sue Ivankovich, Sandy DePorry, and Jean Kulp.

With all the emergency wards he had been to and all of his breathing problems, I know Bill was in a better place. He was a wonderful guy who always tried to do the right thing.

They played country music at his funeral. I'm not a fan of country music, but it fit the situation and made for a respectable service. Jan Allen's daughter also sang a country song. I told Sue and Sandy at the church, and they agreed that the music meshed well with the funeral. God bless you, Bill Perry. He's probably skiing right now where he is.

A signed Willie Nelson acoustic guitar is worth $450.

A pair of 1930 ash wood skis with rubber footplates and galvanized safety bindings is worth $700.

At the June 2012 elections, I ran again for president and was elected along with Dan Worden returning as vice president and, at my request, Eleanor Cheety as treasurer and Eleanor Jenitis as secretary. I kept Doreen Dansky as member chair. It was a great team.

My wife noticed issues with previous BCADA shows and said to me, "You're going to have to run the show!"

I was tired of running shows, but I said to her, "Do I have your blessing?"

"Yes," she declared.

Therefore, in addition to being president, I was also the show chair.

I told the members I would be the show chair, and there were no dissensions, but one member took issue at the meeting. She said it's not in the bylaws and therefore I couldn't do it. She didn't want the job herself but only wanted to be difficult, and other members knew this. I surprisingly kept my cool.

I suggested we make a bylaw change that officers can also be chair people. Of course, years before, Endora Montgomery was president and show chair simultaneously for a long time. This appalled member never came to another meeting and eventually left the membership in 2017.

CHAPTER 20

Our Girls: Emma and Juliet

Emma Rose D'Anjolell was born in 1995. When we were coming up with girls' names, it was an endless list that took us a long time to narrow down. We chose her middle name as homage to my maternal grandmother.

When Karen was barely eight months pregnant, she woke me early in the morning and said, "It's time."

We had only been to one Lamaze class. No bag was packed. I thought, "This can't be happening. It's too soon!"

I said, "It's Braxton Hicks (false labor pains). Go back to sleep."

Karen yelled, "Contractions are close together. Get up!"

I threw clothes in a bag and raced us to the hospital. I needed a *Le Mans* class.

A 1991 white Le Mans Porsche 911 GT1 diecast model by AUTO art, signature series, is worth $225. Note: Le Mans is a twenty-four-hour endurance race that takes place every summer in Le Mans, France.

Emma Rose D'Anjolell was born one month premature. We drove back and forth to the doctor's office many occasions later, but Emma was thankfully normal. She was so funny—constantly taking her toes and placing them in her mouth. We called her, "Emma Rose with the pretty nose and the stinky toes."

Julie & Emma

Her godfather is Chris Ducko. Her godmother is Kathy Hofer who with her husband, Dave, are two of our very dearest friends. Our daughters affectionately call them aunt and uncle. They realize Kathy and Dave would do anything and everything for both our girls.

Artistically inclined, Emma liked to decorate and rearrange furniture at an early age. She enjoyed and devoured lots of books. She wrote for school projects, loved playing soccer, listening to music, and always worked very hard in school.

At Holy Family University, Emma earned the Presidential Scholarship and majored in public relations and marketing. She graduated with top honors—Magna Cum Laude.

An 1898 Haverford College of Haverford, Pennsylvania, wooden box at 7½ inches tall, 7¼ inches wide, and 6 inches deep is worth $120.

Juliet Louise D'Anjolell was born in 1997 with no surprises. Her birth went according to plan. We chose her middle name after my paternal great-grandfather, Louis. She was a thumb-sucker, and after braces, Julie had the straightest teeth in the family. As a toddler, Julie loved to emulate her older sister and follow her everywhere.

A pragmatist who watched her savings, Julie was very good at soccer and was always ready to help others clean up their mess. She maintained a neat and orderly room, liked listening to music, and watched some scary movies. She worked very hard in school and at all of her part-time jobs, which included baby-sitting, as well as working at a auction house called Brown Brothers.

At Delaware Valley University, Julie earned the Presidential Scholarship and the Phi Theta Kappa Scholarship. She majored in accounting like her mother and was on the honors list every semester. Before graduation, she was inducted into the Sigma Beta Delta International Honor Society for Business Management. This was bestowed to only eleven students in the school that year who had earned superior records in business programs.

When the girls were babies, our neighbor Martha DiCredico watched over them during the day while we worked. The girls affectionately called her Mar-Mar. Martha and her husband, John, became good friends. They're also Julie's godparents.

Both girls were showered with gifts from my parents who couldn't help themselves from stopping by our house to get their granddaughter "fix."

When they were young, we took the girls to Disney World where all they really wanted to do was meet all the Disney princesses for the first time. The rides and exhibits were more important on the second visit.

A Snow White & the Seven Dwarfs 1938 Whitman book, Disney authorized edition in mint condition is worth $75.

When they were toddlers, we would play many games and sometimes I would pretend something lived under their beds. I would yell, "Something grabbed my arm under here. I was wrong. There are monsters living under your bed. Run for your lives!"

The girls knew I was kidding, but they would run and yell so loud, it seemed their screams could shatter glass. They killed my eardrums.

Each girl had her share of allergies, and both went to an allergist who found they were affected by almost everything—tree nuts, cigarette smoke, pollen, dog hair, tree sap, and so much more.

One late night, with Julie fast asleep in her crib, five-year-old Emma came into our bedroom yelling she couldn't breathe. I had Karen pick her up and we raced to the master bathroom. I put the shower on full hot water, closed the door behind us, and let the room fill with steam. Suddenly, Emma could breathe. I'm not sure what made me think of that at 2:00 a.m., but it worked. The next day, we were at the allergist when the doors opened. Both daughters have been on heavy allergy medicine all through their formative years.

In elementary school, we had to keep an EpiPen with the school nurse for Emma, as per the allergist, just in case she had an episode.

As they grew older, allergies became less severe, which made it easier to travel with the girls. Karen and I wanted to surround them with as much culture as possible. We took them to almost all the Smithsonian Museums in Washington, the Philadelphia Art Museum, Independence

Hall, Franklin Institute, Natural History Museum, other Philadelphia landmarks, various airplane museums, Gettysburg National Park tour, and Niagara Falls.

A Niagara Falls, New York, dated 1940 pennant is worth $40.

While visiting Boston historical landmarks, we observed Granary Cemetery with the graves of John Hancock, Samuel Adams, Paul Revere, and the man who wrote as "Mother Goose." The girls enjoyed Old North Church, Bunker Hill Monument, Boston Public Garden, the Old State House, and Faneuil Hall.

Niagra Falls 2013

We also watched the Phillies beat the Red Sox at Fenway Park. All of us wore our Phillies colors. The girls liked the food there. It's a beautiful ballpark, as well as the oldest.

A Boston Red Sox 1960s bobble head with green round base is worth $50.

In Baltimore, over several days, the girls enjoyed the National Aquarium and Science Center, the Star Spangled Flag House, Old Baltimore Shot Tower, Fell's Point, Top of the World Observation Deck, Historic Ships at the Inner Harbor, the Baltimore Museum of Art, and then we watched the Phillies beat the Orioles at Camden Yards—another throwback beautiful ballpark, and the food was excellent too. The Babe Ruth Museum, however, was not in the best of neighborhoods, but it was an interesting visit. Babe Ruth was born in Baltimore, started his baseball career in Boston, and became a baseball legend in New York.

A baseball signed by Baltimore Oriole legend Cal Ripken is worth $188.

A clean authenticated Babe Ruth-signed baseball is worth $35,000.

We attended New York city theaters, went to the top of the Empire State Building and of course shopped for clothes. Girls just love to shop for clothes.

A 1954 New York Empire State Building shield design pin is worth $50.

The girls' first Broadway show was *Phantom*. I wasn't sure how they would react, but they enjoyed it. Perhaps just being in the rapid atmosphere of New York was exciting for them.

A framed Phantom of the Opera *Broadway poster signed by the actors, circa 1980, is worth $450.*

In 2008, after twenty-eight years, the girls, Karen and I watched the Phillies finally win another World Series on television. I ran outside in front of my house with my kids running behind me, screaming into the night, "The Phillies are World Champions". Our entire household are big fans and we suffered for so many years in a losing drought. Like a weight off our shoulders.

A Phillies 2008 World Series championship replica ring with faux jewels, is worth $45.

Emma and Julie both worked as a server or hostess at the Havana restaurant in New Hope at one time. As a parent, I thought about some of the creeps who might get drunk late at night and hang at that place or any establishment with a bar in a tourist town. I worried about both my daughters' welfare.

We heard there was a girl Emma knew who bartended across the street from the Havana at John & Peter's Place. This club was known for music and food, and some of my friends had performed there years before. The bartender was in her early twenties and went missing after closing the bar on a cold New Year's Eve night. She lived across the bridge in Lambertville, New Jersey, and simply walked back and forth to work in New Hope.

The story made the newspapers and social media. After she was missing for a week, volunteers including myself gathered at David Rago's Auction House in Lambertville early in the morning along with police officers from both New Hope and Lambertville. We split into five groups of five or six people including one police officer each. Our group was on the Pennsylvania side. We canvassed an area with lots of trees and hills near Windy Bush Road on a cold morning. We came up empty, but a group along the canal on the Lambertville side eventually found her lifeless body. There was no foul play. The police believed that while walking home, she slipped into the icy canal and drowned.

It was a very sad tale for a girl not much older than our daughters and with her whole life ahead of her. This event further made me worry about my children.

Emma and Julie have characteristics that are a little or a lot like Karen and myself. They know how to handle themselves and don't get taken advantage of. That doesn't mean parents still won't worry.

Children change your life. Your heart grows when they are born and become part of your life. You find yourself with new responsibilities and new love to give that you didn't know was within.

A vintage Cartier "Children's Love Bangle" in 18K yellow gold is worth $4,000.

Karen and I are proud of both our daughters and would do anything for our girls. We love that they did achieve excellent marks in grade school through college and know they will excel in the world.

A Tiffany & Company sterling silver graduation cap tassel, ¾ inches in diameter, is worth $150.

CHAPTER 21

The Beatles

I have been a Beatles fan as far back as my memory can go. My parents gave me the Beatles *Something New* album for Christmas in 1964, and I was hooked. I couldn't wait to add more to my collection. Their group albums and solo albums later were a huge part of my adolescence all the way to today.

I never tire of hearing "Breakfast with the Beatles" on Sunday morning radio or Beatle breaks on various radio stations during the week. It may seem crazy, but I've accumulated about four-hundred-plus books on the subject, most of which I read more than twice.

On the night of December 8, 1980, I came home late from working part-time at the Chess King clothing store while still in college. I went to my bedroom and put on my small analog black-and-white television just to have some noise in the background while I changed my clothes. If it was the weekend, I'd move the dial to the old channel 48 and see the tail end of a Basil Rathbone/Sherlock Holmes movie which I loved. But this night, Monday Night Football was on and sports analyst Howard Cosell said, "Oh no, no. I've just been given a report that John Lennon is dead."

I thought I heard it wrong, and he repeated it. John Lennon was murdered outside his home at the Dakota apartment building in New York City. I refused to believe it.

At this late hour, I called my friend Jeff at his apartment in Boston. He was attending Emerson College. Jeff said, "I just heard he was shot. Please say he didn't die."

We were both silent and in shock.

I had a test the next morning at Rider College. As I walked outside toward the building of my classroom, I noticed a banner hanging high from a dorm room window that read, "Lennon Forever." Most of the campus was stunned and eerily quiet. I couldn't concentrate and did horribly on the test. Inside the Rider Student Center, I heard a few girls weeping. It hit my friends hard, too.

I kept thinking about how he finally came out of seclusion after five years, released a good album with *Double Fantasy*, and according to his producer, Jack Douglas, John wanted to tour. I felt with all four of the Beatles on talking terms at this time, just maybe they would have regrouped for a good cause like a cancer charity or something. Instead, this psycho, delusional bastard killed him. My parents couldn't believe the outpouring of people on the streets of New York outside the Dakota apartment building, which included my friend, George Massina. I wasn't surprised by the love and support of the fans.

I was amazed that I couldn't cry over this. I was madder at the gunman than anything, but then my grandmother Rose called me from her home and said, "Are you all right? You lost your friend."

That did it. I couldn't stop crying. She hit a nerve because when you grow up with people you like and admire or anything you care about most of your life, it is like losing a friend.

John Lennon was a big antiestablishment guy, but he knew right from wrong. He gave to many charities quietly. During the late 1970s, he bought new bulletproof vests for the New York City Police Department because he knew they protect us first and foremost. I wish John was wearing one on December 8, 1980.

A John Lennon cut signature is worth $7,000.

The Beatles were the most influential band. Their success was unprecedented. They still rank as the best-selling music artists in history. Eleven of their twelve albums reached number one on the national charts. Lennon and McCartney became symbols of the counterculture in the 1960s. They revolutionized the science of recording with ADT, backward loops ("Rain"), using feedback guitar ("She's a Woman"), and other recording techniques. They expanded the music industry by mixing rock music with folk rock, psychedelia, and baroque pop. They were the first band to receive a Member of the British Empire Award (MBE) from the queen. Rolling Stone named *Sgt. Pepper* the greatest album of all time. They were copied by many but could never be replaced.

"Yesterday" is the most covered song by other artists in history. The songwriting of Lennon, McCartney, and Harrison is influential, copied, clever, and often funny.

Ringo Star was the human metronome. Their producer, George Martin, said no one could keep time better than he. Drummers like John Bonham of Led Zeppelin and Keith Moon of The Who were great hard-rock drummers, but they both stated they wanted to be Ringo.

Rare Beatles Shea Stadium photos sold for $47,000 at auction in 2013.

All of the Beatles great achievements took place in a span of just eight years. There will never be another band like them.

A John Lennon customized Vox electric guitar sold at auction for $408,000.

Mark Lapidos started the first official New York annual Beatlefest in a Manhattan hotel in 1974, and it still thrives today. Mark received the blessing of John Lennon who was already living in New York full-time. Lennon told him, "I'm all for it. I'm a Beatles fan too." All four members of the Beatles donated musical instruments to the charity auction in its first year.

It amazes me teenagers are attending these Beatlefests next to senior citizens, all of them fans of the Beatles in a friendly, happy environment. I highly recommend these events that Mark Lapidos and his family produce.

The first year I went with my friends, Steve and Eric, was 1977 when it was still actually held in Manhattan. It was so interesting to be surrounded by so many people who feel the same way you do about the band. You could strike up a conversation instantly with a complete stranger because you all had a special kinship.

Attending many fests through the late 1970s, 1980s, and 1990s, I met some very interesting people and guests.

I chanced upon Al Brodax who was creator and producer for the Saturday morning Beatles cartoons and producer for the movie *Yellow Submarine*.

A Yellow Submarine movie cell of the blue meanie "Max" at 11 inches x 10 inches is worth $450.

I saw a very quiet Nicholas Schaffner who authored *The Beatles Forever* and *The Boys from Liverpool*.

A 1978 first edition hardcover copy of The Beatles Forever *sells for $50.*

In 1979, I met renowned bass guitarist Klaus Voorman, who met the *Beatles* in 1959 in Hamburg, Germany. He played bass for John Lennon and George Harrison's solo records and for Carly Simon's hit record *You're So Vain*.

That same year, I met New York WPLJ radio DJ Jimmy Fink, who told me a story about an interaction he had with John Lennon. They were in an elevator at his radio station, and John Lennon asked him, "Do you have any gum?"

Jimmy thought to himself, "Here's a guy who has given us so much great music and he asks for gum." Jimmy knew he didn't have any gum with him, but he checked his pockets anyway and said, "Sorry."

Lennon turned to him and said, "I thought all Americans chew gum."

A 1930s Wrigley's Spearmint gum luncheonette serving tray is worth $480.

The March 1981 Beatlefest was the saddest of the all due to John Lennon's death the previous December. My friend Jeff and I saw British actor Victor Spinetti, who acted in the first three Beatles movies. He played the director in *A Hard Day's Night*, the evil scientist in *Help*, and the drill Instructor in *Magical Mystery Tour*. He gave a touching monologue about John Lennon in the grand ballroom of the hotel, and when he finished, there wasn't a dry eye among the huge crowd.

The 1965 Beatles 33⅓ Help *album on the English Parlophone label is worth $50.*

I met Mike McCartney, Paul's brother, known as Mike McGear in the 1960s. He signed autographs and sang one of his songs a capella from his 1974 *McGear* album.

The 1974 McGear 33⅓ album is worth $24.

Singer/songwriter Harry Nilsson had some big hits including "Everybody's Talkin.'" He signed autographs at the fest but only if you donated to his charity. His music was loved by the Beatles, and he became a good friend to John Lennon.

The Harry Nilsson 33⅓ Pussycats *album featuring John Lennon is valued at $25.*

I also met author Ray Coleman, photographer Bob Gruen, and John's first wife, Cynthia Lennon, who were all promoting recent book releases. Singer Billy J. Kramer who was part of Beatles manager Brian Epstein's stable of artists sang with the house band.

The 1964 Billy J. Kramer & the Dakotas 33⅓ album called Little Children *is worth $20.*

Andy White was the session drummer when producer George Martin replaced Ringo for the first single the Beatles released called "Love Me Do." Ringo was not happy about it and reminded George Martin for years after it happened. Andy was very humbled to be at the Beatlefest with his small part of Beatles history.

The 1962 Beatles 7-inch single of "Love Me Do" with sleeve featuring Andy White on drums and Ringo on tambourine is worth $66.

One year, with George Massina and some other friends, Charlie and Diane, we heard the band Badfinger perform in the large ballroom. They were incredible. Badfinger was one of the bands that the Beatles signed to their new "Apple" label. They had several hit singles in the 1970s including "No Matter What," "Come and Get It," "Without You," "Baby Blue," and "Day After Day." We saw them later having dinner at the hotel restaurant and bought them drinks. They thanked us, and we thanked them for the music they made. They were an enormously talented bunch of guys.

A Badfinger "Maybe Tomorrow" 7-inch single created for the Japanese market with picture sleeve is worth $250.

In March 2012, Karen and I took our two daughters to an official New York Beatlefest at its new location, the Crown Plaza Meadowlands Hotel in Northern New Jersey. Emma met Mickey Dolenz of the Monkees who had a long line of people to receive his autograph. Both of my daughters love the Monkees and have seen all the television episodes thanks to DVDs. Emma and I got to the front of the line after waiting for thirty minutes, and she handed a program to Mickey. Mickey said politely to her, "Where would you like me to sign it?"

Emma was sixteen years old at the time and star struck, so she couldn't talk. I said to Mickey, "Right there is fine."

Then I needed to take the frozen Emma by the arm and move her away for the next person to get an autograph. Although she never spoke to Mickey, Emma will tell you her favorite part about the Beatlefest was meeting Mickey Dolenz—classic fan.

A Mickey Dolenz signed autograph is worth $35.

The long-time tribute band affiliated with the Beatlefest, Liverpool, always did a great job replicating the sound. They didn't shy away from performing the harder songs either. In 2012, Liverpool's first song was "A Day in the Life." This song moves into two different keys and is not easy to play, but they performed it with zeal. The girls loved it. You know the band has the right crowd when they get a standing ovation.

The Beatles Sgt. Pepper 33⅓ vinyl picture disc record is worth $40.

CHAPTER 22

July 2012: Dad Dies Suddenly

When my father retired, he saved a lot of money and took our family of six—my two daughters, my parents, my wife, and me—to Italy for two full weeks in 2006. It was so expensive that I knew Karen and I could never afford this type of trip with our kids.

Using a Parillo tour, we stayed in architecturally beautiful hotels, ate at authentic local restaurants, and traveled to fifteen cities including Milan, Lugano (Switzerland), Lake Como, Verona, Venice, Lido, Padua, Florence, Pisa, Naples, Sorrento, Capri, Pompeii, Vatican City, and finally Rome. We loved that every restaurant on the tour in every city had great food. The buildings like the Duomo in Florence and St. Peter's Basilica in Rome were phenomenal—just an architectural dream to experience. Our daughter Juliet had her picture taken on Juliet's balcony in Verona, modeled after Shakespeare's famous tragedy *Romeo & Juliet*.

Our tour had interesting fellow travelers including a Mets fan, of all people, where we made sure he and I tried not to discuss baseball. Looking back at our scrapbook from this vacation, we couldn't believe how lucky we were to have visited there.

Italy 2006

A Vintage Venetian Carnival doctor mask with large feather Pantalone is worth $300.

The island of Capri may have been my favorite. It has incredible views. Everyone was so friendly in Italy. It's as if they actually like Americans.

Someday, I would love to go back again. Our last city before we flew home was Rome. While in Rome, near the Spanish Steps, we went to Trevi Fountain. Like the old folklore says, we threw a coin using our right hand over our left shoulder to ensure we will return to Rome in the future. I hope so. It was the ultimate vacation of my life, thanks to my parents.

A vintage Venetian Murano glass center bowl is worth $120.

A view from the top of the island of Capri: priceless.

My father and mother were very proud of their family. Because Karen's parents died at a young age when our kids were toddlers, my parents were the only grandparents my children really had or remember. Karen and I have no brothers or sisters. Therefore, we were a very close-knit immediate family of six.

My father loved to visit the kids and always wanted to know or help with whatever Emma and Julie were doing. He was a big part of their lives and would proudly show off their pictures to all his friends or anybody who would allow him. Being a grandfather suited him more than anything he ever did in his life. He told stories to them about growing up in West Philadelphia, about their great-grandfather, their heritage, music, wine, food, and his time in the Navy.

During the last few years of my father's life, my mother developed dementia and my father took care of her. It started the year after we returned from Italy. He refused to place her in a nursing home because he felt they would be negligible in their care. He looked after her day and night. This took a big toll on him and caused a lot of stress, which we believe eventually made his newly diagnosed colon cancer worse.

I drove him to St. Mary's Hospital on a Monday. The three doctors who I spoke to would operate on Tuesday and seemed to know what they were doing. I called them the "Three Wise Men." They said he'd be walking out of there on Thursday. My father was dead on Friday. Now I called them "The Three Stooges." Those doctors said there was nothing they could do. The cancer had spread all over his body. Those doctors should have never told us, "He'll be walking out of here on Thursday."

Everyone thought it was not a "big deal" operation based on the initial prognosis. To say my entire family was in shock was an understatement. My father's younger brother, Robert, was in absolute denial. Most of our friends and relatives couldn't believe it either. It was toughest on my children. The entire ordeal didn't make sense and seemed surreal to me.

Many sympathy cards poured in from friends and family. I had to find a nursing home for my mother while I was managing the upcoming BCADA show. I was getting contracts from exhibitors, calling newspapers for the advertising, and managing other related details for a show that was to take place in a few months.

I was very busy. In a strange way, it distracted me from the shock of my father dying so quickly. I dove into the work of managing the show and still exhibited at other antiques shows during this time as well.

Our family had to manage getting my parents' house in order to sell quickly and get out from paying all the utility bills and other expenses. It was a big headache working on this house during a very hot July, especially when the air-conditioner decided to die at the same time.

Karen, our daughters who were in high school, and I would spend eight- or ten-hour days trying to clean up the house, throw out lots of trash on trash collection day, and go through every document in my father's home office. We wanted to be thorough in case there was anything important or anything that needed to be paid off. We were tired, upset, cursing, sweating, and crying over the whole ordeal. No one had expected my father to die.

When we finally arrived home, our little Bichon Frise, Nicky, would greet us at the door as if to say, "My favorite humans are home." After a tough day, he was a welcome sight. He would give us all hugs and undying love. It made these days working at my parents' house just a little bit easier. We only had Nicky since November 2011, and my father loved him. I never saw him so enamored with a dog before.

Nicky arrived from a breeder in St. Louis to the Philadelphia Airport. We couldn't just adopt a dog from a pound because the girls were allergic to almost everything. Bichons don't shed and are hypoallergenic dogs. The whole family took to him so well. He surely is a big part of our family.

My wife says I'm just like him. Nicky makes noises when he's hungry. So do I. He gets excited when he goes out. So do I. He likes to be scratched in his special regions—you get the idea.

Karen and I love dogs. Our friend and fellow BCADA member Chris Wise had a girlfriend who once worked for the Bucks County SPCA in Quakertown, Pennsylvania. When we learned they needed a new heater for the room where the dogs are kenneled, we bought a new mobile heater for them. Why did we do this? It seems like the more people we meet, the more we love dogs.

An antique cast iron coal-fired water heater, 19 inches tall, 14 inches wide, 14 inches deep, made in Pennsylvania, is worth $375.

We used Alderfer Auction and Brown Brothers Auction to unload most of my parents' belongings from their home. My father had a huge collection of wine and spirits in the basement displayed throughout the room. He didn't drink that much but loved collecting hard-to-find bottles of scotch, gin, whiskey, wine, and other spirits. Most of these bottles were valuable. In Pennsylvania, I learned you cannot sell wine and spirits at auction unless the containers are sealed, and then only certain auction houses will touch it.

Auctioneer Brent Souder of Alderfer's did an excellent job, bordering on brilliant, of auctioning more than five hundred bottles of spirits because he stretched them out over six different auctions. This was to avoid bidder wear out. If there is too much of one genre to be sold at auction, the items will not sell as well. The bidding customers will tire of too much of one category.

The liquor sold for more than expected but obviously not retail prices. My parents' other items brought fair prices. These items included about sixty Spanish Lladro figurines, which sold for less than what they were purchased for back in the 1970s thru the 1990s. This is true of any collectible today.

A LLadro medium-size "Bride and Groom" figurine sells for $25.

I also had to hire a remediation company to rid the basement of mold. My parents let the basement go the previous four years as my mother progressed with dementia. My wife and I had no idea the water entering through the basement walls from severe storms had been left to mold and had not been cleaned up. The remediation company was a little expensive but necessary.

The remediation employees were amazing. These guys were born in Serbia and Croatia, countries that became sworn enemies. I said to them, "I'm glad all of you get along."

The supervisor responded, "We are fine. Don't listen to CNN."

Thank goodness no one saw them change into hazmat-type suits in the garage before cleaning out the basement. The neighbors would have called the police to find out what in the world was happening in that house.

They did such a good job, you could eat off the basement floor. I gave each of them a large bottle of champagne from my father's stock in addition to their fee. Just a great bunch of guys—and they all get along!

A 1979 bottle of Bollinger Grande Annee champagne is worth $545.

My friends Dave and Wayne also helped fix a few things in the house before the realtor sign went up, including a ceiling patch, and they helped clean out the garage attic.

My parents' house was sold within two months thanks to my realtor friend Brian Pawlowski. All of the revenue from the house sale and contents of the home went to cover the nursing home expenses for my mother in Doylestown. Medicaid took over when that money ran out, which was within four years. It went fast.

A vintage "Open House" two-sided steel realtor sign, 32 inches x 6 inches, is worth $150.

My wife and I felt so strange and sad during the holidays with my father gone and my mother in a nursing home not remembering who I was anymore. The tight family unit was down to four. Karen and I had some kind of depression, which I think is the price you pay when you love someone who is gone.

My father, like myself, was a big Phillies fan, and trades were exciting to see if the team improved. For months, whenever a Phillies trade happened, I picked up the phone to call Dad to see what he thought about the trade and then realized he was gone. Birthdays, anniversaries, and holidays were never the same.

A 1975 Bell Systems model rotary telephone is worth $110.

CHAPTER 23

The November 2012
Hurricane Antiques Show

We had another show scheduled in November at a school in New Hope. I was happy the show was completely filled and all the advertising and postcards were in place. Unfortunately, we were clobbered by Hurricane Sandy on the East Coast, causing floods and power outages.

With one week to go, I called the head of building and maintenance at the school to cancel the show due to the storm. The school was relieved because they thought they might have to call us to cancel.

It was a blessing we did cancel because on that show date of Saturday, November 3, there was no power at the school and PECO used their parking lot as a substation for many of their trucks. I know this because I drove down there and was forced to take back roads because Main Street (Route 32) in New Hope was closed due to flooding.

I got a call from a member who told me he saw quite a few people waiting in line at the school thinking there was a show. Already upset that we canceled the show, I lost my patience with this guy.

I said, "What are you asking me? That we should have had the show with no power at the school and most of the main surrounding roads closed?"

He has a hard head like a coconut!

A vintage Marx Brothers "The Cocoanuts" poster, 42½ inches by 27½ inches, is worth $70.

We returned half the rent back to all the dealers after we received the rental check from the school. The dealers were OK and understanding about the whole debacle. However, we spent and lost all the money on advertising and marketing. It was a big waste of time and money with no recourse.

Meanwhile, the school had other thoughts for us for the following year in 2013. They wanted to place in writing that we have patrons pay for parking, and I told them NO, thank you. Time to find another venue.

———————— ♦ ————————

We did have some outstanding speakers at our BCADA meetings in 2012. Joy Harrington discussed her expert knowledge and love of antique dolls with some rare examples.

An antique German bisque head wood body, 21 inches tall, is worth $80.

Member Erik Fleischer told a passionate story about the true inventor of the steamboat, John Fitch, who lived in Warminster, Pennsylvania, at one time. Erik helps run the John Fitch museum on weekends and gives great tours.

An 1850 Mississippi steamboat canal route Thomas Cowperthwait map is worth $100.

Member Bob Lucas discussed his expertise on nineteenth-century photography with examples from his valuable personal collection. Bob's knowledge is well known, and on occasion, he serves as a consultant to auction houses.

A nineteenth-century picture of a gentleman cabinet card by Davis Photography Studio is worth $20.

Member Dan Worden taught us his wisdom about sterling silver and silver plate items. Dan is the expert for silver, without question.

A pair of Gorham sterling silver candlestick holders, 10 inches tall, circa 1910, is worth $200.

Guest speaker and my friend Mike Schwartz explained his comprehensive knowledge on antique glass bottles with personal examples.

An 1870 glass "Old Sachem Bitters & Wigwam Tonic" bottle, 9¾ inches tall, as-is condition, is worth $65.

Guest speaker and friend Tony Lee discussed his wide-ranging knowledge on political pinbacks. He is fair and honest and may be the most renowned authority on the East Coast.

A 1904 Roosevelt & Fairbanks political pinback button is worth $95.

Member Stanley Smullen shared his extensive knowledge on antique weapons. In my view, Stan is the ultimate expert who exhibits at many weapon antiques shows.

A Civil War model 1840 cavalry sword with scabbard is worth $450.

In 2012, we added new members including James Curran Antiques & Restoration in Lambertville (British antiques and furniture). I have purchased some of his restored furniture, and you cannot tell what's been fixed. He and his staff are excellent with any kind of furniture that needs restoration.

A nineteenth-century George III Pembroke table, circa 1810, is worth $600.

We also added Ted and Linda Freed of T & L Antiques based out of New Hope, Pennsylvania (books and ephemera). Ted has excellent knowledge about old books and their publishers.

A 1949 Frank Baum Ojo in Oz book with dust jacket is worth $105.

We also welcomed new members Isaac and Sara Abir of Serapi Antiques based out of Huntingdon Valley, Pennsylvania (oriental rugs, pottery, jewelry, and silver). Isaac is an authority on Oriental rugs, and he and Sara both are very kind, down-to-earth people.

A 1941 Roseville Pottery "Columbine Pattern," 10-inch-tall vase is worth $90.

Scott and Elsie Tagg of Factory Antiques in Silverdale, Pennsylvania (furniture and primitives) were also added as members. Their store in Silverdale, Pennsylvania, is one of the best in Bucks County for any genre of antiques. Elsie has an amazing Pinocchio collection, with a good portion from Venice, Italy.

An antique Yoke Oxen Harness with metal rings is worth $90.

Liz Billies and Roger Bordman of Cook & Gardener in Lahaska, PA (china, glass, art, majolica, fishing, and hunting) also became members. Their excellent store has unique finds located near Peddler's Village in Lahaska, Pennsylvania.

A 1930s Bamboo Saltwater Fishing rod by Heddon, number 144 model, is worth $140.

Author and member Patricia H. Burke based out of Pt. Pleasant, NJ, is an excellent writer and antiques dealer (primitives, china, glass, silver, and decoys). She wrote an excellent authoritative coffee table book called *Gerald Rutgers Hardenbergh – Artist and Ornithologist.*

A mid-twentieth-century hand-carved Madison Mitchel blue bill Duck Decoy is worth $100.

My State of the Union speech at the December meeting spoke mostly about how the show was canceled due to Hurricane Sandy. I also needed to explain what the school had planned for us in 2013 with extra fees we certainly didn't need.

The school also refused us to use our new large show banner because it was against their policy. They were going to charge us $300 to keep the free parking for patrons. We needed to get out of there.

I learned there was a new landlord at the New Hope Eagle Fire Hall named Cornerstone, mostly known for their health clubs. It was time to investigate this hall, especially because we needed a new venue.

On the upside for the year, I loved our secretary, Eleanor Jenitis, for the way she wrote our newsletter. Eleanor Cheety was a great treasurer. Dan Worden, as vice president, was perfect for giving an objective opinion. And the members seemed to want me as president.

A 1904 presidential campaign Theodore Roosevelt tapestry rug is worth $500.

CHAPTER 24

Back to the Eagle Fire Hall in 2013

After ten years of running my own antiques show at the Eagle Fire Hall, ending in 2011, I found myself back there in 2013 with a new landlord named Cornerstone. They assured me they would do everything to help us with our annual BCADA show. I secured a contract for the second weekend of November, which became our usual time for the annual show.

Cornerstone also did an excellent job of refurbishing this large catering hall. It looked fantastic. My floor plan was good enough for thirty-two exhibitors, but we would be packed in like sardines.

An 1880s English majolica basket weave-style sardine box is worth $300.

After our show, we had our usual end-of-the-year December dinner party. I was careful to thank all our volunteers, our exhibitors, and those members who promoted the show to help make it successful.

One of the stories from that show involved a red-haired older woman who wanted someone to appraise an item from a cell phone photo. I informed her it's always difficult to appraise from a photo and not proper for an appraisal. Using a photo of an item to be appraised is

BCADA show

not wise because you can never fully see any condition issues first-hand. She persisted in not a polite way and kept bugging me while I was with several customers trying to write up sales. When she mentioned furniture, I passed her to Steve Cheety, who knows furniture well and because I knew Steve would absolutely not want to talk to this lady, which I found very funny. The woman approached Steve with her whole story. Then Steve pretended he didn't speak English. He passed her across the aisle to Alan Snyder who gave this lady his time and felt sorry for her. Steve told me he would have rather taken shrapnel.

I later told Alan, "In the words of Alexandre Dumas, 'You are the best of all of us, D'Artagnan.'" Alan was the only person who took the time to speak to this woman while the rest of us were too busy with customers.

An 1898 Alexandre Dumas two-volume set of The Three Musketeers, *illustrated, is worth $295.*

Some people don't realize that exhibitors have paid to be in a show and this is a business, not a public service for their specialized needs. This woman could have taken a few minutes to arrange a future time to bring in her item to a qualified appraiser with the actual item and not a photo.

For the first time, after hurricane-affected shows, "old guard"-run shows, and unpleasant school shows, we finally had an excellent antique show with very few glitches. I was happy with the outcome.

A vintage Happy Trails Roy Rogers on Trigger watch is worth $70.

A Show booth

CHAPTER 25

Good Speakers, Good Show in 2014

I had found some interesting guest speakers including Tony Lee who returned to discuss political and ceremonial ribbons. Tony taught us a great deal, and I would highly recommend him to anyone needing information in his area of expertise.

A Henry Clay 1844 ribbon with elegant imagery, slogan, and portrait is worth $700.

Guest Bob Garay talked about antique tools and used many within his own collection to explain the story.

A rare, vintage double-clawed hammer (used for better leverage) is worth $150.

Guest Amy Perenti, head of appraisals at Freeman's Auction in Philadelphia, did a terrific job of discussing what was happening at their auction with regard to the effects of today's antiques market on their sales. She told us, "Middle-market furniture and newer item sales are flat, but if the item is rare or has provenance, it will sell very well."

Provenance is the chronology of the ownership, custody, or location of an object, and it always adds value to the item.

Member Ashley King spoke about clocks and his many years in Germany learning about clocks and watches. Ashley is a great speaker with a voice that's a cross between actors Wilfred Brimley and Robert Duvall.

An 1870 Seth Thomas mantle clock with wood case is worth $300.

Guest Bruce Updegrove, a former schoolteacher, cleverly described World War I using the covers and titles of sheet music in a very entertaining way. He detailed the public sentiment before, during, and after the war. Our club loved his presentation.

World War I-era sheet music with beautiful illustration sells in the $5 to $15 range.

The October meeting was a first of many to follow with presentations by members who discussed what they collect. At this meeting, I spoke about my Phillies yearbook collection, and my wife, Karen, discussed her teapot collection while providing examples. Her earliest was a nineteenth-century ironstone teapot worth about $150.

A common 1940s English Sadler teapot in mint condition is worth about $30.

We added some new members including Scott and Debra Vombrack of Old Dog Antiques (furniture, advertising, lighting, ceramics, and jewelry). They are two honest and dedicated people who love finding, discussing, and selling antiques.

A 1930s "Green Spot Orange Soda" door-push advertising sign is worth $120.

Russ and Judy Miller of Ironmaster's Mansion Antiques (Staffordshire, maps, art, and Native American) also returned as members. Russ and Judy are lovely old-school antiques dealers who love the way the club is headed. They are very personable people and a joy to be around.

A nineteenth-century Staffordshire Historical Blue "Franklin's Morals" transferware serving platter is worth $250.

Also returning were Priscilla and Al Naylor of The Very Thing (Oriental antiques, sterling silver, and tin toys). They always have beautiful-looking booths and are simply a touch of class in every show. Maybe the club was doing something right with former members coming back to the fold.

An early twentieth-century tin toy red Coca-Cola truck with original coke bottles is worth $150.

We inducted a new treasurer, Ted Freed. Eleanor Cheety held that post for two years but became busy with her family. I totally understand that family comes first. She did a great job.

Ted Freed had recently fallen out of a tree and landed on his back. Consequently, his retina became detached and he'd had problems with this eye ever since to the point that he couldn't drive anymore. His other eye had been inoperable since birth.

I drove him to Alderfer's Auction in Hatfield, Pennsylvania, on most Thursdays for which he is forever grateful. I also made him run for treasurer because it gave him something to do. He still had enough eyesight in the damaged eye for close-up work.

I think Ted felt he was useful to the club, and he did a good job, sometimes seeing notes in bills to be paid or bills we'd already paid that I didn't catch.

———— ♦ ————

The 2014 show went well. We had a little over six hundred patrons, who truly liked the show. My exit interview from patrons went like this: "Didn't read the paper but saw the signs outside"; "the meatballs were slightly undercooked but the show was great"; "prices seemed fair"; "I came back the second day"; and "great selection of antiques."

Another show rule: every show needs a food caterer to keep them in the building. Don't allow the patron to leave simply because they are hungry. The longer they are there, the more likely they will buy.

An early twentieth-century wide hand-forged spatula is worth $125.

It was a good show and we discussed its success at the December holiday meeting. There was an issue, however, with one member who wanted to do our show but her husband was against it. She called or emailed me throughout the spring and summer constantly asking what her booth size was. Then finally with a month before the November show, told me she had to cancel because of her husband's demand and didn't expect her money back this late.

She wasn't getting it back that late anyway. I switched into gear and started calling dealers with only weeks before the event. Most said they couldn't exhibit at that time because they had other plans that weekend. It's difficult to add someone a few weeks before the show.

Luckily, member Bob Lucas stepped up and said he would do it, and we had a full venue again, which I announced at the October BCADA meeting, only a couple weeks before the show.

This woman attended the October meeting and emailed me that night when she returned home late and said, "Since we have a dealer to fill my spot, I want my booth rent money returned."

I lost my patience, and I lost my temper. Anyone planning to go to bed in my household that night heard me in our home office. I responded back with a very long, detailed email to her without any curses. I informed her about every time we spoke or emailed throughout the year, what she said, what I said, the weather outside my office window each time, the clothes I wore those different days, if my dog was sleeping in my office or not, and so on. I especially mentioned how many times I told her not to do the show and that she would have had a complete refund at that time. Therefore, no, she wasn't getting a refund.

There wasn't a response back. When the "dues notices" were emailed out to members in early January 2015, she emailed me back with a short note to say, "I am not returning to the club." It wasn't because she didn't get her booth rent back, but because her husband didn't like the tone of my last email to her back in late October.

This lady is a very sweet soft-spoken person. God knows I tried, but I was fresh out of patience with her. Yet maybe I could have been more understanding, especially with older members of our club. I felt like it was more my fault than hers. However, people like that drive me insane.

An 1886 paper receipt from an Asylum for the Chronic Insane is worth $35.

CHAPTER 26

The Death of Ginny Lovekin

Original member to the club Ginny Lovekin died on June 23, 2015, of old age. When her daughter Sherry Steigerwalt called me late that night, she started the conversation with, "I was wondering when the day would come that I had to phone you with this message."

Instantly, I knew what she was going to say.

Ginny carried some of the best Native American items anywhere. It was great having her as an exhibitor because she was the only person carrying that type of merchandise with no overlap from another dealer.

Native American antique merchandise can be quite valuable; for example, a 13-inch-tall Hopi Pueblo Kachina doll is worth about $500, a Hupa Indian basket is worth about $1,000, and an early Blackfoot Indian beaded vest is worth about $800.

This part-Native American woman was always in my corner. She said to me, "Keep doing what you're doing." These words kept me going during some dark days in this club. She was ninety-plus years young. Once in her booth, a man told her an item was too expensive. Ginny responded dryly, "You don't have to buy it," which had made me laugh.

We had a moment of silence for her at our first meeting after the summer in September with her daughter Sherry and her amiable husband, Ernie, in attendance. I was happy to see that Sherry wanted to continue as a member because she and her husband are both awesome people.

The 2015 show had a dedication for Ginny on the back of our customer handout. Sherry was exhibiting at the show, but it wasn't easy for her without her mother after all those years together at BCADA shows. Sherry did walk over to me at the show and whispered, "Keep doing what you're doing. I know my mom would want me to say that to you."

The 2015 show was well attended with almost six hundred patrons. The look of the show was outstanding with members outshining what they did the previous year, although it was very sad to not see a mainstay like Ginny exhibiting at the show. She will certainly be missed. I will miss her acerbic but charming wit and her "two cents" at meetings.

An 1866 U.S. uncirculated two-cent piece, MS-64 grade, is worth $149.

Friday, the show setup day had its share of buying between exhibitors. The biggest recipient was Doreen Dansky, who had already made her rent and more on Friday selling to other dealers. She sold an arched pair of shutters for several hundred dollars. Vintage arched shutters will always bring more value than shutters that are flat across the top. Arched shutters are rarely made with today's modern windows. People like to decorate with these shutters outside and inside their homes.

An antique pair of wood arched shutters, 82 inches in height x 32 inches in width, is worth $400.

Many exhibitors sold well including Craig and Helen Smith who had a large booth with nineteenth-century furniture and accessories. Julia Bartels's partner, Hank, sold three of his four eighteenth-century men's vests to one buyer. My friend Lori bought a large quantity of items from Bob Lucas's Civil War merchandise. Bob was very happy and thanked me both days for making sure Lori attended the show.

A Civil War-era "U.S." insignia Union army belt buckle is worth $200.

Patrons' comments to me included "eclectic show with quality"; "I was at the Elverson show on Saturday and everything looked brown.

Part of my 2015 Show booth

This show looks much better"; "prices were reasonable"; and "great show, see you at the next one." I was very pleased with what the patrons thought about the show and all our exhibitors.

By the end of the year, we added the Smiths of Temora Farm back to the fold as well as new members, Dick and Barbara Spahr.

The Smiths sell fine period furniture, artwork, and metalware. They are two long-time previous members with hearts of gold. They quietly help people who have fallen on difficult times but never publicize their actions.

A nineteenth-century "Prancing Horse" metal doorstop is worth $50.

The Spahrs sell original art, Staffordshire, Ironstone, and Flow Blue china. The Spahrs are two charming dealers with impeccable taste in their merchandise.

An original oil painting of Loch Lomond in Scottish Highlands *by Francis E. Jamieson (1895-1950), frame size 20¾ inches x 28¾ inches, is worth $600.*

It was a good year for the club except for losing Ginny Lovekin. However, there was one couple who wouldn't stop complaining about the club, how the show was run, and everything I did. Those people were a husband and wife who complained about their booth location, what they thought were not enough signs outside, and so on. They would tell their feelings to anyone and everyone who would listen.

As president, I'm the face of the association. They never once took me aside to voice their opinion and only shared their opinion with everyone else. It went on for months and months. I heard all about their complaints from other members because I'm "Father Confessor." Everyone feels they need to enlighten me, whether good or bad. But also, the antiques world is a small community. Everyone hears about everyone's co-ops, how they did at a show, what's selling, and so on. We didn't need this kind of negative publicity. If they were kicked out of the club, then finally they'd have a reason to whine.

The officers and I had enough, and we drafted a certified letter stating that we would not accept the husband and wife's dues for the new year.

I waited until after Christmas. In a letter dated December 26, 2015, we mailed back their dues and stated some of the above reasons for revoking their membership. At the January meeting, we took a vote, and it was unanimous.

I took a long pause after asking, but no one at that meeting came to their defense.

A World War II Civil Defense helmet with missing paint and dried-out chinstrap is worth $50.

CHAPTER 27

Downsizing and How I Hate Food Poisoning

In July 2015, we sold our large home that we loved and downsized to a townhouse still in the community of Newtown.

We had lived in a four-bedroom home with a finished basement totaling more than 3,500 square feet of space. My wife and I always felt that someday my parents would move in with us. However, with my dad having passed away in 2012, my mother with serious dementia now in a nursing home, and our oldest daughter moving out to live with friends, there were only three people living in the house including our daughter, Julie, and of course, our dog, Nicky. The house and the property were too big for us, but I actually loved the setting and our neighbors.

After much discussion, we decided it was time to downsize. With the help of our friends Martha and John, we had found a great mover called Broderick Moving Company based in Feasterville, Pennsylvania. This company is careful, thorough, and inexpensive. I would use them again if needed.

A 1960 toy Mayflower Moving truck, 13 inches in length, with original box, by the Marx Toy company is worth $350.

The night before the close, we needed to stay overnight in a hotel that took dogs because of our little Bichon. A hotel called Elements in Ewing, New Jersey, not far from Newtown, was perfect for Karen, Julie, Nicky, and me. All of our home contents were safely inside the moving truck. We just needed some supplies for the overnight stay.

An Art Deco Grand Hotel Eden luggage label from Lugano, Switzerland, is worth $110.

Although our hotel did not have a restaurant, the desk clerk in the lobby informed us that across the street, there was a Courtyard by Marriott with a small bistro. We ate dinner there. All of us had the chicken Caesar salad and then returned to the Elements hotel.

That evening, Karen was violently ill in the bathroom. Later, in the middle of the night, Julie was also sick. By now, we knew it had to be the food. I knew I was next. Our dog watched us with concern. How do they know?

Then it was time to wake and get to our closing appointment on time with our realtor and buyers alongside us, the sick people. We told our realtor what had happened and he said, "Don't tell the buyers. It could jinx the sale of your house."

He had made a good point. The buyers might look at it as some kind of grave omen before moving in. We needed to put on our happy face to survive the morning closing of the sale. It was not easy to say the least.

At the closing, the buyers were asking all kinds of questions that could have been solved more than a month earlier, and we needed to depart soon to meet our moving company.

Finally, our terrific realtor, Brian, made Karen sign what was vital and then she headed to the new home with Julie. I stayed behind at the realtor's office with the buyers, while I periodically dashed back and forth to their bathroom. I looked like death as many around me felt compelled to tell me.

A 1943 Ray Bradbury signed Death Is a Lonely Business, *first edition book is worth $50.*

When Karen arrived at our townhome, Broderick Movers had already started getting our possessions into the house because the last time someone was there, they didn't lock the door properly, allowing access to the home. One of the first things we did after we settled in was purchase a proper new doorknob and lock.

When I arrived, a pale-looking Karen and Julie were half slumped on chairs and pointing for these wonderful movers where our belongings needed to go. Broderick did all the work; we didn't carry anything nor could we. The movers were impressive.

In the middle of all this, I finally used the master bathroom for the first time and got violently ill as Karen had been the night before. My throat was so sore; I needed to see my family doctor, who declared I ripped a small hole in my throat from this episode. I could only drink warm liquids like tea for a while, and it finally healed itself.

A vintage Nepalese Buddhist hand-hammered metal healing bowl, 9 inches in diameter, 5 inches in height, is worth $290.

After eventually calling that horrible restaurant and explaining our plight, they merely told me, "Sorry." Where's the health department when you need them?

I miss our old house and the neighbors, but it was the right time. We are paying one-third of what we paid before on utilities, and more importantly, we no longer have a mortgage. It also made it much easier to pay for the girls' college tuition and travel wherever we wanted.

A vintage Delaware Valley University embroidered jacket is worth $75.

CHAPTER 28

The Alan Goodrich Murder

Doreen Dansky, our member chair, and I often seek out really good people who are antiques dealers to add to our association. Two of these people were my friend, Alan Goodrich, and his son, Eli. They had exhibited at my old Bucks County Antiques Show. For many years, they exhibited with great primitives and eclectic merchandise and always an impressive-looking booth. Customers always commented on how much they admired their merchandise. Alan and Eli both had an incredible knowledge of primitives and country furniture. Besides selling locally at shows, they loved to sell in the huge outdoor Brimfield Shows in Massachusetts two or three times per year, and they usually sold very well there.

They once had an intact early twentieth-century Halloween costume displayed at my show for only $200. It was definitely underpriced.

I said to Alan, "That seems it should be worth much more."

He said, "I don't want to live with it. I want to sell it."

That is a good standard for any antiques dealer to use.

Halloween started out as a Celtic New Year celebration. At the start of the twentieth-century, Halloween was an adult festivity with tons of folklore. The Hallows Eve legend stated that on that night women could stare into a mirror and see the reflection of the man they would marry. There are pre-1915 Halloween postcards representing this legend.

Early Halloween postcards in excellent condition today run $15 to as high as $400 for a mechanical Halloween postcard. Today, Americans spend more than $8 billion on Halloween items and candy annually.

Alan was a former English teacher at Neshaminy School District in Bucks County. When he retired, antiques became a full-time business for him. For some reason, former teachers are the largest group of antiques dealers, more than any other vocation.

I spoke with Alan about joining one day in 2013, and he said that he was just not a joiner. He quoted the Groucho Marx line that he "wouldn't want to be in a club that would have him as a member."

A Groucho Marx signed photo is worth $900.

However, Alan said at some point, "I'm going to slowly retire, and my son, Eli, will take over the business. He may be interested."

Eli, always hardworking for his father, was a pleasant, quiet young man. I spoke directly with Eli at an auction about joining the BCADA and he said, "Sure, that sounds good." I told him that Doreen Dansky, our member chair, would interview him on the phone, and he gave me his cell number.

Doreen attempted to reach him several times over the next month and would always need to leave a message. I contacted Alan who said Eli may have changed his mind. Of course, Eli could have told us that.

Two years later, on August 4, 2015, I couldn't believe what I was watching on television during the evening news program. Alan Goodrich, age sixty-seven, was murdered by his son, Eli, age twenty-six, in the peaceful neighborhood of Langhorne, Pennsylvania. The report said the father and son argued. Eli screamed, "You can't control my mind anymore!" Then he left the house to walk his dog. He returned and told his mother he loved her, then went into the other room, picked up a sword, and stabbed his father in the chest. Alan was pronounced dead an hour later.

On June 29, 2016, the court hearing stated Eli Michael Goodrich, a mentally ill man, fatally stabbed his father, Alan Goodrich, with a "Zelda sword." He was sentenced to serve 17½ to 45 years in state prison. Eli suffers from schizophrenia. He pleaded guilty but mentally ill in Bucks County Common Pleas Court to third-degree murder and possession of an instrument of crime. Judge C. Theodore Fritsch, Jr. accepted a negotiated plea agreement in which attorneys recommended a sentence of fifteen to forty years for the murder and a consecutive two and a half to five years for possession of an instrument of crime.

Alan Goodrich bled to death after his son thrust a sword through his abdomen while the elder Goodrich was sitting in a chair in the TV room of his Langhorne home. The weapon, a "Legend of Zelda" sword patterned after a popular video game, was coated in blood the entire length of its blade.

The court also said that Eli Goodrich, who alternately regarded his father as his "best friend" and "the devil," claimed he succumbed to voices in his head instructing him to commit the murder. Among other delusions, he had accused his father of raping his mother, his fiancée, and his dog.

Goodrich's lawyers were preparing to present an insanity defense if the case had gone to trial. A psychologist and a psychiatrist for the defense had concluded that Goodrich was legally insane at the time of the killing.

Deputy District Attorney Marc Furber, however, said he was prepared to prove that Goodrich did know that his conduct was wrong at the time of the crime and thus did not meet the legal criteria for insanity.

At the hearing, Eli, who cried during much of the hearing, said to Judge Fritsch, "I'd just like to say that I loved my father. He was great to me. I never would have done this if I had been in the right state of mind."

In accepting the negotiated plea, Fritsch called it a "very difficult case. It's a case involving mental illness (and) the tragic death of a well-loved father."

To Goodrich, the judge added: "It's clear to me that you have great remorse for what you have done." He said he would recommend that Goodrich be sent to the State Correctional Institution at Waymart, which specializes in handling prisoners with severe mental illnesses.

After the hearing, we learned more details about what had happened the day of the murder. Middletown police had been summoned to the Goodrich home shortly before 5:00 p.m. Officers found the victim sitting upright and dead in his chair, with his shirt soaked with blood. With him were his disabled wife, June Goodrich, and his son, who surrendered immediately. The sword lay on the floor beside a nearby sofa. An autopsy determined that the sword had severed an artery, causing death within two to four minutes of the attack.

After being handcuffed, Eli Goodrich told police that he was a regular marijuana smoker who had just quit cold turkey and that he had been up the entire night before drinking coffee. He said that he had smashed his cell phone because he suspected people were spying on him through it, that billboard signs and Netflix shows were about him, and that he took showers in the dark so that he could better hear the voices that spoke to him.

Eli Goodrich, an English and communications graduate of St. Joseph's University, lived in Philadelphia with his fiancée and planned to be married at the end of August 2015.

His mother told police that her son had come home earlier in the day, retrieved the sword from upstairs, and brandished it at his father. Eli Goodrich told his father that he was not going to let him control his mind anymore and said, "I have to kill you" before leaving with the sword and his dog.

He returned at 4:00 p.m., spoke briefly with his father, and then asked his mother if Alan had ever raped her. She told him no.

Eli Goodrich then returned to where his father was seated and plunged the sword through his body and part of the chair. From the next room, June Goodrich heard her husband cry out and say, "You're going to kill me." Using her walker, she entered the room to find her husband impaled by the sword.

"Don't worry, Mom, it's a fake sword," Eli Goodrich said before re-moving the weapon. He then called his father "Satan" and said his father had raped his fiancée. When his mother asked if he was on drugs, he replied, "I must have gotten some bad weed."

The shock of the scene caused Mrs. Goodrich to fall and fracture her back. Eli Goodrich then ran through the house, looking for a knife with which to kill himself. His mother convinced him to stop.

Later, under questioning by police, Eli Goodrich said that he and his father had a good relationship, despite occasional arguments over student loans and his mother's health care. He said that he knew it was wrong to kill his father. Goodrich told police that the voices in his head had tricked him into committing the murder. The last thing he heard the voices tell him, he said, was that his father was not the devil, that they "got" him, and finally, "Checkmate."

This story reverberated throughout the BCADA membership because so many people knew Alan. Members were shocked because this sort of thing doesn't happen around here.

Doreen and I wondered what might have happened if Eli had become a member of the association. I felt sad for the whole family. It was such a horrible tragedy.

A vintage Alcatraz Prison porcelain sign, 15 inches x 12 inches, is worth $180.

CHAPTER 29

The Improved 2016 BCADA Show

Speakers in 2016 included Brent Souder of Alderfer's Auction, who discussed art. Member Ashley King discussed how the United States gave away the watch industry to the Swiss. Member Erik Fleischer talked about his shaving mug collection, which today has dropped in value with vintage shaving mugs selling as low as $10 to $30. Member Alan Snyder discussed his collection of Cape Cod and Nantucket memorabilia.

A 1960 Nantucket basket purse made by Stephen Gibbs, with traditional carved whale on mahogany plaque, is worth $2,000.

Returning guest speaker was the wonderful Bruce Updegrove, who lectured us about German spiked helmets of World War I. I couldn't believe how heavy those spiked helmets were. These soldiers ran into battle wearing a helmet weighing twenty pounds or more.

These helmets are valued at $150 for a World War I German spiked Helmet Pickelhaube to $900 for a World War I German Felt Prussian Army spiked Helmet Pickelhaube.

The 2016 show was excellent with 609 patrons in attendance. Many exhibitors did very well in sales.

However, we had a security breach during the show. Two elder gentlemen decided to browse the show on Friday. They snuck in through the storage area door. I had to escort them out. Of course, they acted like they didn't know it wasn't OK.

A new caterer, Kathy's Catering, made the best homemade chicken pot pies. They sold a large quantity during the show with some customers bringing them home for dinner later. Kathy sold out of them by the end of the show.

A 1910 silver-plated dome roll top catering server with removable bowl is worth $130.

Two of our nonmember exhibitors, Gary Block of G. Brooks Antiques (eclectic antiques, advertising, and metalware) and Lynn LoPresti of Hickory Springs Antiques (furniture, primitives, and country) decided they wanted to join our club. They both had great-looking booths and are retail oriented with their customers—they understand service management. We added both dealers in early 2017.

Gary Block, a very hospitable antiques dealer and schoolteacher from Delaware, carries eclectic antiques and is always a positive individual. He has a lovely wife and children who are as charming as Gary.

A large vintage wooden chicken crate carrier box is worth $200.

Lynn and Pete LoPresti, very considerate people, had an array of fine primitives, vintage fireplace cookware, and furniture. They informed me that they had a better show than they expected. Based on my observations, I believe this was due to the fact that they catered to their customers, had reasonable prices, and knew how to make their booth look enticing.

A Show booth

A Hepplewhite New England drop-leaf farmhouse table, circa 1820, is worth $900.

Early 1800s Hessian Andirons with rare blue-painted coats are worth $1,500.

An English copper coal bucket, circa 1850, is worth $600.

One little conundrum occurred a few weeks before the show. A garish man called me to ask for a booth, and I explained how we were completely booked. His response was, "So, I can't get into the show?"

"No, sir."

He grunted, "You won't let me in with my excellent merchandise?"

I said, "We are completely booked. There is nothing I can do but place you on our waiting list."

He angrily said to me, "I am coming to the show on that date to kill you," and then he hung up.

I instantly called the local police, told the story, and gave them his particulars that I had attained—his phone number, first name, and his business (which was listed on my phone). I asked the policeman what my options were.

The policeman couldn't have been kinder. He said, "Do nothing. I will call this man and tell him if he comes to the show, he will be arrested and placed in jail. And call the New Hope police as well to keep them informed."

I called the New Hope police, who wrote down the man's particulars and said they would have a patrol car by the show those two days and to call them if anything happened.

I was less concerned about my safety than I was about this person causing a disturbance at our admission table and therefore preventing patrons from entering the show or simply frightening people, including our volunteers.

The man never showed up, and the show had no issues. It also turned out to be the best-looking BCADA show to date. How can you top this? Well, we did the following year.

A rare best-looking Gucci 7100M wristwatch is worth $255.

CHAPTER 30

March 2017: Mom Dies

My mother was in a nursing home for almost five years as she gradually got worse from Alzheimer's. It was a horrible way for her to live. She didn't know anyone anymore and became afraid of everything. I would visit, straighten her room, and talk to her but received complete silence in return. We all prayed that God would take her away to be with my father. It was a horrible way to live, and I told my wife, "If I get like that, hit me in the back of the head with a shovel when I don't expect it."

On March 25, 2017, I received the call from the nursing home that she had passed. I felt she was no longer living in the nightmare world of dementia. All her friends who were still alive kept saying they were sorry, but it was a blessing.

I gave a eulogy at our church in Newtown. It's a very small United Methodist church with beautiful stained glass from the Civil War era. I had a closed-casket funeral because she looked so frail and thin at the end. I wanted people to remember her the way she was and therefore had photos of her from when she was younger. The eulogy I gave went something like the following:

Mom circa 1960

"My mother grew up in a close community in the Tacony section of Northeast Philadelphia. It was primarily an Italian, Irish, Polish, Catholic community where everybody knew everybody. When she married my father in 1957, they needed to move to Jacksonville, Florida, near the naval base where my father was stationed. When he was discharged, they moved back to Tacony where I was born in 1958. My mother worked as a dental nurse for more than thirty years. When I came home from school (*Our Lady of Consolation,* which no longer exists), I entered an empty house from an unlocked back door, and there were never any problems. I would do homework until my parents came home around six p.m. My mother would make dinner after a long day at the dental office, then wash and iron clothes, and get the house in order. On Saturday, she would clean the house from top to bottom and go out with my dad to dinner, or see friends, or a movie. On Sunday, my mother usually cooked a big meal served in the dining room with family, friends, or neighbors. On Monday, it started all over again. We always had music playing in the background on a big stereo mahogany console (aka the record player), all day long. All kinds of music—popular, opera, Bossa Nova, big band, jazz, crooners, rock, and other music. When on vacation, my parents loved to travel—Spain, Portugal, Italy, anywhere with wine country. On weekends, they might head to my grandmother's Brigantine, New Jersey, shore home and have family and friends for dinner there.

"Growing up in an Italian Catholic family, there was passion, music, crying, laughing, and sometimes yelling. But at the end of the day, there was always love and food. My mom was the one who kept the family unit together. After I married Karen, we had two beautiful daughters, Emma and Julie. Amazingly, my mother quit smoking cold turkey so that she wouldn't smoke around the kids. On certain days of the week, she would watch our girls while my wife and I worked, and she would teach them songs on the piano and watch classic movies with them like *Wizard of Oz* and *Sound of Music.*

"What I miss most was when I was about eleven years old, I was in a big play at Catholic school where I played a photographer. They gave me a big box and painted a camera on it (get it? Box camera). I told my mother I was nervous, and she said those perfect words: "It will be OK." Mothers have this special power that no one else has. They should all be in *The Avengers*.

The play took place, the audience liked it, and I was fine—nothing to worry about. I think that's what I miss most. When your mom says, "It will be OK," it's magic. Everything just gets better. I miss you, Mom."

An Art Deco "Brownie" box camera by Kodak is worth $80.

CHAPTER 31

The Marvelous 2017 Show

We started 2017 with forty-four members after we added Gary Block of G. Brooks Antiques and Lynn and Pete LoPresti of Hickory Springs Antiques. Great people!

We also increased our membership with Paul Gratz, an art conservator and gallery owner based in Doylestown. He is the best at conserving an original painting, not just in Bucks County but anywhere. When you conserve a painting, you add value to the work. Paul Gratz is the best!

An antique oil-on-canvas picture of a Clipper Ship, *unsigned, 12 inches x 18 inches, is worth $125.*

Jane Ashton, who is my long-time friend and who deals in furniture, was added to the club. Like me, she is a big Phillies fan who loves to help people and has reasonable prices on her furniture.

A primitive country farm table with white scalloped edge and drawer, 62 inches long and 30 inches wide, is worth $900.

Also added was Bob Smith, Alan Snyder's friend, a hardworking fine gentleman who deals in mid-century modern items, which are desirable today. Bob gives the club a boost of energy on Friday—the setup day for every BCADA show—by helping out.

A mid-century modern round copper top Egyptian-style coffee table is worth $200.

In 2017, we had member speaker, Dan Worden, talk about vintage corkscrews, which are very hot sellers right now.

A vintage Sterling decorated Stag handle corkscrew is worth $50, while a vintage Syroco French Bulldog corkscrew is worth $90.

Greg Glemser, a local gemologist and jewelry dealer out of Doylestown, discussed the latest with jewelry. The high value of gold and silver usually trumps the value of who the manufacturer is; this is known as scrap value. Therefore, jewelry value comes down to the value of the gold, silver, or platinum. Add more value if it has a diamond or other precious stones. Greg is the go-to guy for jewelry and a member of the Pennsylvania Antiques Appraisers Association.

Excellent returning speaker Joy Harrington talked to us about vintage dolls using many from her own collection.

An 1870 black cloth doll with good clothing, a defined nose, and authentic hair sells for $1,000.

A 1790 English wooden doll, carved and jointed, with glass eyes is worth $4,000.

We had a wonderful picnic in 2017, although my wife wasn't there. She had to care for our sick dog at the vet. Our wonder dog, Nicky, turned out OK.

The same officers and chair people were in place as we moved forward into a big unknown in the antiques business. More and more genres just weren't selling. Members were changing some of their stock to fit the times, and we had no idea how many people would see us in our show.

For this 2017 show, I decided to add Radius magazine, a small local Bucks County magazine. They wrote a genuinely good article about our show. I always write the yearly show articles for media. Then those editors use a portion in their papers. At Radius, the editor wrote a great piece of literature about our show that was thankfully larger than a postage stamp.

An 1879 three-cent brown postage due stamp, in mint condition, is worth $48.

We also did a commercial with the help of my daughter Emma and that great voice of member Ashley King. Ashley was perfect as the narrator. I wrote the commercial script, used pictures from the previous year's show, and included background music from a movie. It was a minute long and aired all over social media. Our webmaster, Sue Ivankovich, added it to the home page of our website. The best part was that people told me they saw it.

Our setup and breakdown crew for the last few years has been the best. This crew includes both of our porters, Dave and Wayne, Assistant Show Chair Jack Taylor, members Bob Smith and Chris Wise, Karen D'Anjolell, and me. We all do specific jobs on Friday setup before noon when exhibitors can move in their merchandise with porters, Dave and Wayne.

A vintage Sheraton Hotel metal porter badge, circa 1950, is worth $35.

After the 2017 show closed on Sunday evening, we had the highest

Exhibitors getting their booth ready

attendance since 2005 with 756 patrons; total gate in 2005 was 807. I was ecstatic. It actually seemed like we had about one thousand customers because we were always busy with a constant flow of people walking around the show. It was as if nobody wanted to leave. Fifteen customers returned on Sunday and as usual were not charged again for an entry fee. People were still entering the show late on Saturday and on Sunday with only a half hour left before closing on each of those days. This amazed me.

The Amazing Spiderman #1 comic book in near mint condition (CGC 9.8) signed by Ryan Ottley and Erik Larsen is worth $1,500.

We had rave reviews from exit interviews I conducted with patrons. There was not one negative response. One person said they "loved talking to the dealers about the merchandise." Other comments were, "Best show in Bucks County"; "looks great"; "very diverse"; "I bought a lot today"; "show is well put together"; and more than once, "Thanks for having the show." Those who submitted this latter comment could have been grateful because there are simply fewer shows everywhere.

A woman said our "marketing was phenomenal" because she saw an ad in the *Doylestown Intelligencer,* saw an ad in the *Bucks County Herald,* saw our commercial online, received an email about the show, and received a postcard in the mail from one of our exhibitors. In the advertising business, that's called great saturation.

A 1960 Aquadive brand Saturation Dive watch for commercial diving is worth $3,000.

Members were happy with the results of the show, and most exhibitors sold well. The lovely Isaac and Sara Abir of Serapi Antiques sold better at this show than they did at their last Chantilly, Virginia, show. Ted Freed, Karen Taylor, and the Frazers sold better than they did in the 2016 show. Doreen Dansky and I both had our best BCADA show ever, while Gary Block and Ivan Raupp had the best show ever in their careers.

Don Casto, age eighty-one, had an excellent show and wanted me to make sure that our club members knew this. Don's been doing shows since the 1980s all over the map. He said it was the best-run show he had ever been involved with and he hoped to do the show the following year.

All in all, it was a great year with no problems, issues, or deaths to report. I was very happy. As show chair, I didn't know how I could top this show.

A vintage cast iron top bell for reception desk, circa 1930, is worth $130.

CHAPTER 32

The Millville Incident

At the start of the new year in 2018, I had high hopes after what our show achieved last November. The first show of the year for me to exhibit was the Yardley Antiques Show, which usually takes place on some of the coldest days of the year in mid-January and sometimes with snow. I sold well as did many of our fellow BCADA members who exhibited in that show. The next show, usually at the beginning of February, is the Wheaton Village Antiques Show in Millville, New Jersey.

Wheaton 3-inch-tall miniature presidential glass bottles range in price from $2 to $20.

I always exhibit at the Wheaton Village Antiques Show, which in 2018, fell on February 3 and 4, a Saturday and Sunday, with the setup day on Friday. This antiques show is well run by the intelligent, energetic, and considerate Lauren Wymbs.

An incident happened on that Friday setup day. I went to the local Millville Target store around 3:00 p.m. to buy a six-pack of tall waters for my room at the Quality Inn. The hotel rate is fair, and they give you a hot breakfast each morning. Over the last nine-plus years, it's become my home away from home.

It was still daylight after I left the Target store. As I headed back to my vehicle, I saw an average-sized man in shoddy clothing try to break into my car saying, "I need to get home to West Philly."

I lunged one step forward toward the man screaming, "Get away from my car."

The man took several steps back, and I jumped into my car and sped off. The moral of this story is when you exhibit in a tough town like Millville, be careful when you leave the compound of your hotel or leave the show area.

When I got back to my room and placed the bottled waters into my tiny refrigerator, I had a moment to think about what would have happened if this guy had a helper. Then I was rattled about the whole thing.

An 1890's cast iron water pump marked Beatrice, Nebraska, 45 inches in height is worth $265.

I told this story at our next BCADA meeting in April as a warning for our members but I added that what I should have done, though I only had seconds to think, was run back into the Target store, alert the manager, and have them call the police so that this thug didn't try it on someone else.

Although this incident rattled me, I thought maybe it would be the only terrible event to affect me that year. I was so wrong.

CHAPTER 33

The Death of Todd Dannenhower

Member Eleanor Jenitis and I are like brother and sister from different parents. I love Eleanor and will do anything for her. We talk about music and discuss who is the better band, the better lead guitarist, the better song writers, and so forth. We're close in age, and therefore, with our partners, we often went to dinner, visited art galleries, and just enjoyed each other's company. We were all very close and often discussed many subjects without any boundaries. No topic was off limits.

If I was exhibiting at a show that included Eleanor, who was also an exhibitor, her long-time boyfriend Todd Dannenhower would help her set up her booth. Then he would find me and ask if he could assist in any way. He was always caring and attentive to anyone he helped.

Soon after the Millville, New Jersey, show, on February 7, I received an alarming phone call from Eleanor. Todd Dannenhower, her boyfriend, partner in business, soulmate, housemate, and my friend, had committed suicide.

I never had anyone close to me commit suicide. It hit me like a brick. Todd never ever said anything to me or Karen, nor did he seem to have any suicidal tendencies. I never saw it coming, nor do I think anyone else did either.

Members knew Todd because he always came to the big BCADA holiday dinner meeting party every December since Eleanor Jenitis first joined. Members Doreen Dansky and Jean Rutter, who were close to Eleanor, were shaken by his death and wanted to know why. Everybody wanted to know why.

It was difficult for Eleanor, a very strong woman, to get the words out when she called that day. She said he had been having headaches for a while and was taking drugs to curtail it. He was down a little on himself because his new "contractor" business was taking a long time to start up. Todd told Eleanor at one point, "Maybe I should drop this idea and just get a job somewhere."

Eleanor was looking for him that evening, and it was odd he didn't call. Police found Todd in his truck in a desolate area killed by a single bullet through his head. The police said there was no foul play. They went to Eleanor's house around midnight to inform her and she became hysterical, as most would be. Eleanor and Todd had lived together and were practically married.

There really are no words to console someone over a loved one's suicide. Todd was younger than Eleanor. He was only forty-eight years old, far too young to die.

I told Eleanor if there is anything I could do, please tell me. She just kept saying, "I want my Todd back."

She said they had future plans including going to Canada for a fishing vacation and had updated their passports and fishing licenses. Todd had a dental appointment coming up, a car service appointment, and other errands on their agenda. He didn't sound like someone who was ready to take his life. Experts say that suicidal people usually get their house in order and leave a note. None of this happened. It didn't make sense.

I wondered if maybe the headaches were like a constant migraine that wouldn't go away. Then he shot himself on that particular part of his head to take away the pain, not believing it would kill him. No one will ever know.

The funeral was at a beautiful old Lutheran church not far from their home. It was a wonderful service. Todd's best friend, then his sister, and finally Eleanor all spoke eloquently about Todd after the pastor was finished. Karen and I went to the funeral, and other BCADA members sent cards.

Eleanor brought a picture of Todd in a frame and placed it on the podium facing her as she spoke about how much he meant to her. It was a touching tribute.

Eleanor didn't come to the April BCADA meeting, but she came to my sixtieth birthday party on May 6 and maybe seemed slightly better. She was apprehensive about attending, but I told her, "BCADA members will come up to you and say they are sorry and then they won't bring it up ever again."

Todd was such a good guy and good friend. I wondered if I or anyone could have said or done something to change the outcome. The world lost a great guy.

CHAPTER 34

Turning 60

Even though when I was young, I said I would never turn into my parents, it was too late. When I wake up in the morning, I'm making my father's noises.

A few months before my May 6, 2018, birthday, I had an idea that I wanted to do something meaningful for my birthday and make a difference in some way.

When my father died suddenly in 2012, it rocked our family from its foundation. As I mentioned, my wife and I are both only children. When Dad died, our small nuclear family came to a screeching halt. With the shock of my dad's passing, having to place my mom in a nursing home, and the ordeal of getting my parents' house ready to be sold, we went through some trying times, but our dog, Nicky, was always there to lift us up at the end of a hard day.

This experience had me thinking about how dogs help soldiers get accustomed to being home from war and often help them work through symptoms of posttraumatic stress disorder. There are moments these "service" dogs go to work with their owners to help them cope with their job environment. I thought about those dogs in the armed services that find bombs or evil guys. And I thought about Police K-9 units who find drugs or sometimes save the life of their police partner.

Then I saw former Channel 3 meteorologist and now retired Carol Erickson on Channel 3 News every Sunday morning with a couple dogs from the Pennsylvania SPCA (PSPCA). The dogs appear on the local news program to encourage viewers to adopt them. Carol discussed the dos and don'ts of caring for pets. She did this every Sunday for free. The PSPCA does not pay her. With a family of her own and a grandchild, she could easily be doing something else on Sundays. I felt her precious free time to give to the PSPCA was exemplary.

Carol Erickson's service for the PSPCA, our love for our own dog, and what dogs can do for people all contributed to an idea for my sixtieth birthday.

I contacted the beautiful Washington Crossing Inn to reserve space for a large party, wedding size, on the Saturday or Sunday night of my birthday weekend. They were booked except for a time slot of 12:00 to 4:00 p.m. on that Sunday afternoon of May 6, which is the actual date of my birthday, and I took it.

I invited eighty-four people and called them in advance of the actual invitation to get their perspective on my plan. I wanted no gifts from anyone. Instead, I wanted each person to write a twenty-five-dollar check to the PSPCA. This idea was universally accepted by everyone, and they all said it was a "great idea."

Some people who couldn't make it mailed me a check or mailed one directly to the PSPCA in my honor. I was ecstatic by the response and called the headquarters of the PSPCA in Philadelphia to tell them about my plan and why I wanted to carry out this idea. Ross, my contact there, was extremely grateful and said that Carol Erickson comes to the office all the time. He was going to tell her my story.

Two weeks later, Carol called me to say, "Thank you for helping the PSPCA," and, "I would like to attend your birthday party for a little while." Of course, I said, "No problem."

I reserved my friend Bob Farmer's Beatles tribute band, the Hearts Club Band, for two sets of forty minutes each. I picked all the songs. Bob didn't want to charge me when he heard what I was doing in lieu of gifts, but I insisted on paying the band. Bob's a great guy with a lot of talent like the rest of the band.

Finally, on Sunday, May 6, everyone arrived for a five-course meal with assigned seats just like a wedding. In attendance were my close friends, close relatives, some of my parents' close friends, and close friends from the BCADA, as well as the Washington Crossing Card Collectors Club. I wish I could have invited many of my other relatives and friends, but the room was only so large and we filled it.

At about 12:30 p.m., Carol Erickson arrived, and I asked the band if I might address the now-seated crowd. I told them the whole story about Carol and how she devotes so much time to the PSPCA since she retired from television. Then I introduced her. She addressed everyone and discussed the PSPCA and everything they do for the community including going after the depraved people who condone "dog fights." Carol is as pleasant and wonderful in person as she appears on television. She is a role model for people who have the time, patience, and passion to give to a worthy cause. I can't say enough about her. She is also interested in antiques.

Later, I made it a point to tell the audience, "I practiced singing the Beatles song 'Birthday' in my office with the song blaring out of my computer speakers and me belting it out, but I couldn't hit the high notes like I could ten years ago. However, since it is my birthday, and you can do whatever you want on your birthday, I'm going to sing it anyway."

Carol Erickson

The audience erupted in laughter, and I sang it. The band was perfect, and I thoroughly enjoyed myself. Several people recorded me singing on their cell phones. I will not quit my day job.

It was a great party with delicious food that was covered by *Bucks County Herald* photojournalist Michelle Alton, who must have taken one hundred photos. Fourteen of these excellent photos were print-ed in the *Herald* with the story two weeks later. Michelle did a great job, and she also donated a check to the cause—very sweet of her.

A 1969 Paul and Linda McCartney autographed wedding photo, 8 inches by 10 inches, with COA, is worth $3,700.

My friend Eleanor Jenitis sat at my table. It was very hard for her. However, Eleanor told me at the end of the party that she spoke with some BCADA members. Sometimes talking can be somewhat therapeutic. I hope it was.

So many people I love were there besides my wife and kids, including my godfather Benny and his wife, Fran, my Uncle Fritz and Aunt Maryann, Uncle Vince and Aunt Jean, and some of my cousins who I love to pieces—Dana, Angela, and Dana. Good friends George and Jackie, Joe and Donna, Dave and Judy, Mark and Karen, John and Martha, and Bart and Jenny were all in attendance. Besides Eleanor Jenitis, other close friends from the BCADA attended.

Plus, friends from the Pennsylvania Antiques Appraisers Association (PAAA) attended, in particular Ashley King and Dan Worden and their partners. Friends from the Washington Crossing Card Collectors Club including retired army colonel Bob Snyder all the way from Missouri who flew in just for the event, plus Heather, Susan, Joe, Rich, Bruce, and Marj, all were there as well.

Like they said in *Magical Mystery Tour*, "A splendid time was guaranteed for all."

The Beatles Magical Mystery Tour *album from 1967 vinyl LP, still sealed, is worth $225.*

CHAPTER 35

Teaching at Delaware Valley University

My friend and fellow BCADA and PAAA member Ashley King started teaching antiques classes at Delaware Valley University in New Britain, Pennsylvania, during the spring session of 2017. New Britain is sandwiched between Doylestown and Chalfont, Pennsylvania.

Ashley has a big heart and loves to talk and banter with students—or anyone for that matter—about antiques. He has a kinetic energy that people warm to when he teaches. With his knowledge of different genres on antiques, he is an absolute expert on clocks and watches. While in the Air Force, he spent more than ten years in Germany, which is when he began his education on the subject of clocks. Like me, Ashley loves to talk to students. He is also the go-to guy to fix or clean clocks and watches.

An English eighteenth-century oak Tall Case Clock by John Worsfold, 78 inches tall with rosewood star on door, single weight, and square brass dial is worth $4,700.

Ash invited me to more than a few of the classes to teach students on a variety of topics that I could choose myself. It surprised me how much I actually enjoyed the interaction with these adult students.

One topic I covered was:

"What to do when you visit an antique show, antiques store, or flea market."

1. Make a list of what you're looking for because you can easily get distracted with all the items you see.

2. If you're with a companion, bring your cell phones and use them like walkie-talkies in case you split up over a large venue to inform the other person when you've found the item you're looking for.

3. Wear comfortable shoes for walking a long distance and perhaps bring a bottled water.

4. Bring a loupe (a small magnifier) to tell markings on an item (e.g., to determine if a piece of silver is sterling or silver plate or the signature of an artist, etc.).

5. Bring a small measuring tape or ruler. This is handy if you are looking for furniture or a large piece of art and the location in your home or office has only so much space. It also saves you from taking a trip home to measure and then return to where you saw the item. A small one fits in your pocket easily.

6. Bring cash or checks. Many outdoor market vendors will not accept credit cards. At stores, this should not be a problem. Also, when you use cash, you may get a better price. Don't expect ATMs to be nearby.

7. Get there early! The best items are first come, first served.

8. Set your sights on items that are in perfect or near-perfect condition because they will hold their value much better.

9. If you see exactly what you want at a fair price, get it now! Don't go back later when it could be gone. "If you snooze, you lose!"

10. If you're not sure if it's real or a fake and the price seems extremely low, don't buy it because it's probably a fake. Go with your gut feeling.

11. If a dealer seems like they are exaggerating the truth and that something doesn't seem right about the item, just walk away and don't bother to buy it or discuss it further.

12. If the price is close to what you want to pay, gently ask the dealer for his best price. Never ask a dealer to go less than half of their asking price. They will be insulted, you will not make a transaction, and you could possibly be verbally abused.

13. If you're not sure about an item, ask the dealer what they know about it. They will usually inform the buyer everything they know because they want to sell it.

14. Lastly, don't forget to have fun. That's why we hunt and collect!

I've taught his students on several occasions, as well as to various groups at libraries, town halls, churches, and synagogues. It's interesting how many people are so curious to learn about antiques. I receive different questions at every class and am surprised how much the average person does not know.

An antique German brass magnifying glass with brown Bakelite handle, 8 inches long, is worth $195.

CHAPTER 36

Collecting George Washington

People in general always ask me what kind of items are selling in the antiques business. There are various items selling to collectors, gift buyers, and the occasional antique purchasers. One of the genres that I sell is George Washington memorabilia. George is still the most popular president ever followed by Abraham Lincoln and Teddy Roosevelt—in that order. He is the father of our country, leader of our first army, and our first president. He did not, however, chop down a cherry tree. This folklore helped to teach children to never tell a lie.

Today, George is selling better than ever. Items include not only real autograph signed personal letters that are expensive, but especially less expensive items with his name or likeness.

These items range from the nineteenth century to the early twentieth century and include:

prints and paintings of George (with or without Martha); military, police department, fire department, and political ribbons or pins; flags, banners, quilts, and other textiles; re-election posters of other politicians that include Washington's face; sterling or silver-plate utensils, silverware, souvenir spoons, and jewelry; glass bottles, decanters, and tumblers; ceramic mugs, figurines, souvenir plates, vases; and andirons, metal urns, and clocks.

Most major ceramic manufacturers created merchandise with George Washington's picture, but they vary in price. For example, a 1910 Rowland and Marsellus English ten-inch souvenir plate depicting "Washington crossing the Delaware" will sell for eighty dollars. However, a 1920 Taylor, Smith, and Taylor china company ten-inch "George Washington" souvenir plate will sell for ten dollars. It's not the ten-year difference in age that made the price vary between the two, but rather the quality and beauty instilled by the earlier English company makes it more superior.

Differences in art also affect the price. For example, a nineteenth-century small-framed silhouette of George Washington can cost $300, while a much larger lithograph of George's face, circa 1932, will only cost $90. In this case, the difference in value is the rarity of the silhouette.

The year 1932 was big for George because it was the two hundredth anniversary of his birth year. Many companies made souvenir items in praise of George that year. It was also the first-year coinage of the U.S. Washington quarter.

Numismatists have coveted the new Washington quarters that on the flipside have all fifty states. There were five different quarters per year, dating from 1999 to 2008. These quarters are popular among collectors in proof sets as well as uncirculated editions.

True collectors of George Washington items tend to gravitate to the much older items. However, I have found that designers who are employed by owners of country-style homes, inns, or restaurants couldn't care less about age, but rather, they consider the condition, size, and color as the more important criteria for their project.

If George Washington were alive today, I think he would be most flattered and humbled by those who admire him.

A July 3, 1797, George Washington signed letter revealing how he intended to free his indentured servants when he left the president's house (there was no White House yet) is worth $50,000.

CHAPTER 37

Managing an Antiques Show

When I look at antiques shows that have been fixtures for many years, they occasionally lose their legs. They are no longer as vibrant. Often, the show promoter is on automatic pilot and doesn't try to improve the show every year, or perhaps the location of the show has become destitute. Sometimes the overwhelmed promoter aims to do better, but if they fell down, they'd miss the floor. Here are some tips for managing a successful show:

1. Finding a venue is never easy because there is so much involved in the process, specifically for antiques shows. The show needs to be in a town that has a high household income. Check the average value of a house in the area. This could help patronage from people who live nearby.

2. There needs to be ramps or no steps to enter the main floor of the building. This helps for easy access in and out for exhibitors, as well as handicapped customers. It's preferable to have the show on a first floor unless there are elevators like the Philadelphia Convention Center, but this is rare.

You don't want too many ways to enter the main room for the show because of security concerns. If thieves think they have a way to break in, they will do it. And it is beneficial to have a security alarm system that encompasses where the show is held.

An antique Rockwood Sprinkler company cast iron alarm Bell Cover from Worchester, Massachusetts, 40 pounds, 19 inches in diameter, is worth $225.

Schools are not the best choice, yet I exhibit at many of them myself. The problem with schools is that a show promoter contract with a school or group sponsoring the show doesn't mean anything. That's because the school answers to the school board or the PTO.

For example, if a school board or PTO decides they are going to all of a sudden charge for parking, then the show promoter is stuck. Patrons for the show will get irritated if they have to pay for a parking fee at the school and then pay again to enter the show. Patrons could be millionaires and most of them will still feel they are being taken advantage of.

Schools may change the date regardless of whether you have event promotions printed using the original date for the show.

Another example of why using a school can be challenging: there was a long-running indoor show in Bucks County at a private school. It was an elegant, large old building with much history, making it a fine setting for a show. The promoter warned there was going to be a heavy rainstorm during the weekend of the show. Cars needed to park on the grass field because there wasn't enough room for patrons' cars on the asphalt parking lot every year at this venue. The rain was a big downpour that lasted all day. After the show, the grass was torn up by the cars trying to leave the show. The school went ballistic because they had to replace the multiple mud patches with new sod. This incident ended this wonderful annual show. There was nothing the promoter could do to change the school's decision.

A Show booth

There was a long-running show at a large Catholic school cafeteria in Montgomery County, Pennsylvania. After this annual show ran for many years, the pastor decided there wasn't enough parking for his church patrons during the Saturday evening mass. Although the show brought in quite a bit of money for the parish from booth rentals, the food concession, and the customer gate, the pastor ended the show forever.

A Victorian Eastlake walnut Catholic church pew, 34 inches tall and 48 inches long, is worth $340.

3. A large fire house hall, large hotel ballroom, large VFW hall, or large catering hall are the best choices because your contract will stay binding and not change.

Once you have achieved a venue, stay on good rapport with your landlord. Always make sure your down payment (or full payment) to rent the hall are on time. There is absolutely no reason to be late because your landlord is the deity who determines your future at the venue.

An early twentieth-century Frank Lloyd Wright-designed Imperial Hotel, Japan, menu is worth $260.

4. You must have insurance from a reputable company to cover any show. Most venues will demand it.

An early 1900s brass National Union Fire Insurance company sign, 9 inches in height and 15 inches wide, is worth $250.

5. Promoters need to know their business. There was a school in Moorestown, New Jersey, that held an antique show every year. Running the show were a group of very pleasant people who were extremely helpful, but they did not know the antiques world. They would simply sign up people for the show and have no clue what kind of quality merchandise the dealer had or what genre. Therefore, the show started to contain too much jewelry and too much junk. The show lost many regular customers and quality dealers. Then, the show committee decided to add craft dealers with new merchandise, making it easier for them to maximize exhibitors. This was the kiss of death, and now the long-running show no longer exists. Antiques enthusiasts and new crafts buyers are two different kinds of people and the two should never mix.

A new needlepoint on canvas of Mt. Vernon, *12 inches in height and 10 inches in width, is worth $15.*

A 1901 Mt. Vernon *print in a yard-long frame is worth $110.*

6. Promoters need a solid list of reputable dealers promoting quality merchandise—one needs to add worthy dealers each year to the exhibitor waiting list even if the list is already long. Keep the list fluid because prospective exhibitors change their minds, retire, move away, or die. Just as an antiques dealer is on the hunt for quality merchandise 24/7, so should the promoter of a show scan for quality dealers 24/7.

The more the better, but never promise a new exhibitor there is space available if you're not absolutely sure. The promoter needs to keep that list handy because right before the show, an exhibitor may get sick, have a family emergency, or all of a sudden simply can't do the show.

A 1920 English hunt scene framed print, 13 inches in height and 13½ inches in width, is worth $200.

7. Keep your dealer contract simple and to the point. Treat all dealers the same just like you would the patrons who come to the show. There should be no favoritism for anyone.

If the show booth rental is low (i.e., less than $250), the exhibitor should pay the whole amount with the returning contract. If not, you need to always get a deposit from the dealer or they may easily change their mind down the road with no loss to them.

Don't be held hostage by a dealer if their demands are different than the contract. Tell them, "Sorry, but this is how we run the show." You don't need an exhibitor like that because it sets a precedent you don't want.

A vintage Police Hostage Negotiator megaphone is worth $250.

8. When you mail out or email a contract to a dealer whom you haven't spoken to in a while, get in touch with them. If it's a small show (i.e., less than forty exhibitors), it would be advantageous to give all the dealers a phone call first before you mail or email anything to them. This will also inform you if they are still interested in exhibiting at the show, are not retired, and you're not wasting your time later.

An 1846 property contract of the Pratt Estate in Charlestown, Massachusetts, is worth $250.

9. Have a reliable setup and breakdown crew who are thorough, smart, steady, and trustworthy. Train them well to complete all responsibilities before exhibitors arrive. Make sure they treat all exhibitors the same.

The entire crew needs to be on time to finish their task before you open for dealers to set up. If setup time is noon, dealers will be there at 11:55 a.m. You can count on it.

A 1947 English Crew paddle trophy from King's College is worth $450.

10. Porters need to be careful with exhibitor merchandise. They should think every box they handle has glass in it. And they shouldn't ask for tips; the tips will come, or let the promoter handle it. At one of my old shows that I managed, an exhibitor named Joan did not tip the porters for a couple years. The porters were afraid to tell me because they thought I might kill her. When it finally came to light, I spoke to Joan and she acted like she had no idea. I banned her from exhibiting at any show I manage. There was no excuse. This woman had tons of merchandise and tied up one of my porters for several hours every show! This long-time veteran dealer knew what she was doing, and it cost her.

A vintage Porter Sunkist wooden crate, 12 inches in height, 12 inches in width, and 13 inches deep, is worth $85.

11. Admission table teams need to be careful with quick-change artists and use a special marker to determine false currency. Have plenty of change for the admission table. If it's a two-day show, have change for both mornings.

12. Advertising should be a combination of local newspapers and magazines along with trade papers and trade magazines. Also use social media like Facebook and Instagram. There are also many free calendars on websites. If you don't advertise with a particular paper or magazine, check if you can be placed in their calendar section. Readers might look at the calendar part of a paper more than the ads.

With smaller newspapers and magazines, it helps to double check about a week before with your contact to make sure they have everything they need before they go to print. One instance: I contacted a small paper to make sure our ad was all set. My account person said, "I'm so glad you called. We can't find any of your information." These are people who are not necessarily organized and could never obtain a job with the *Wall Street Journal* or *Washington Post.*

Make sure your advertisement pops. You want people to notice! Include fewer words, but include the what, where, and when.

An 1891 advertising iron scale, 13¼ inches long, for New Yorker farm magazine is worth $500.

13. Develop a mailing and emailing list for each show with a signup sheet at the admissions table. As this list grows, periodically clean the list to make sure the addresses are still valid.

Mail out postcards from your mailing list about twelve days before the show to your regular patrons. This gives your customers plenty of time to place the date on their calendars yet not too early before the show where it could get lost.

Make sure your exhibitors have as many postcards as needed. They will hopefully mail postcards to all their special high-end customers and anyone else they deem worthy.

Canvass your postcards to stores within a thirty-mile radius. It doesn't just need to be antiques stores but also art galleries, coffee shops, hotel lobbies, and bank and post office information boards. Always make sure you have consent from the manager. If not, your postcards may end up in the trash. Postcards work! Of all the media used for advertising, most patrons come to the show with a postcard.

An antique wooden primitive Post Office sign for West Lebanon, Maine, 14 inches in height and 47 inches in length, is worth $275.

14. You need to have a food refreshment area in the show if the hall doesn't provide one. If your show opens in the morning, patrons may need two to three cups of coffee to wake up, especially the exhibitors and the dealers who visit. The food caterer usually doesn't make a ton of money at shows because patrons may stay for only an hour or less. But you need them there anyway, particularly those patrons who stay at the show for hours. They get hungry and thirsty. Of course, some shows are known for their good food, and patrons look forward to it. Just make sure your caterer has fresh food so no one gets sick.

15. It helps, if possible, to have soft music playing in the background during a show. Like a supermarket or mall, shoppers are more at ease with subtle easy-listening music playing in the background. They mostly won't remember what song they heard, but it will relax them enough to feel comfortable to shop.

The Carpenters CD box set is worth $16.

16. Evaluate the show each year as a guide to determine what worked and what didn't work because you always have room for improvement.

At the end, always thank your exhibitors for being there. Without them, you can't have the show.

When I ran my Bucks County Antiques Show for ten years, I learned a lot over time and listened to patron comments. This is a must.

Actress Blair Brown visited the show in 2004. She starred in films with William Hurt (*Altered States*), John Belushi (*Continental Divide*), Clint Eastwood (*Space Cowboys*), and other A-list actors. Ms. Brown scans antiques as she slowly walks around the venue. She is a big collector and frequent visitor to antiques shows. She told me, "This is a very good show with quality antiques."

When you hear this from a collector, you're going in the right direction.

CHAPTER 38

Millennials

The antiques business is a very tough vocation, and today's "Millennials" or "Generation Y" mostly couldn't care less about antiques. Millennials are anyone born from 1980 to 1998.

This group has been closely watched by marketing firms and retail corporations about what makes them tick because they are a large part of the population that buys countless flavored drinks, cell phones, laptops, software, and so on. They are very tech savvy.

Most of them enjoy music, computer games, social media, spending time with friends, shopping online, watching television, going to the movies, and eating. Eating translates to eating out at restaurants, bars, shopping centers, take-out venues, or a fast food drive-thru. Most do not use the kitchens or dining rooms in their respective homes. Therefore, they don't care for dining room furniture or fine china sets, which have driven those values way down. They would think a gravy boat is something you use on the water.

A vintage Atari CX-2600 video computer system in original box is worth $285.

My realtor friend who is based out of New Hope, Pennsylvania, told me he had a small townhouse to sell in the area. He said usually young people buy these as their starter homes before they move up to something bigger or better. He told the owners to take all their dining room furniture out of the house. The dining room was right next to the living room and he spread out the living room furniture, created a new floor plan, and called it "the great room." Young adults loved it.

When I asked him, "What do Millennials want in a house?"

He said, "Updated bathrooms and updated kitchens."

Yet they don't use the kitchen much. However, because they don't stay too long in a starter home (two to four years), when they resell it, the bathroom and kitchen are already updated—very smart.

This group likes to work, likes to make money, and likes to save money. Many like to move into the city they work in, to be closer to work and closer to the places they tend to frequent. When they live in the city, they get rid of their car and save money on maintenance expense and auto insurance. They get around using mass transit, Uber, and Lyft. This also means they can drink late and not worry about driving home.

When it comes to shopping, they like new things; they prefer to buy online, using cell phones, and Amazon is their friend. Antiques are something their grandparents liked. Millennials like today and tomorrow—not yesterday. This attitude affects antiques, as well as all the collectibles that you ever heard of. After the 1990s, the collectible market had crashed. This market included items like Hummels, LLadro figurines, Royal Doulton jugs, stamps, Avon bottles, McDonald's glassware, Matchbox cars, and magazines.

A 1981 complete set of four McDonald's drinking glasses from "The Great Muppet Caper" is only worth $10.

Therefore, antiques dealers cater mostly toward people ages forty and older because today's youth rarely wants what we sell. We need to constantly recalibrate our stock to accommodate what we think is actually selling. We can't excessively get into one genre if tastes change. It's a tough business.

Both my daughters are millennials and they like new things, they purchase items online, and they use their phones incessantly. I told them, "If you buy something from Pier One Imports, Crate & Barrel, or stores like those, don't tell me."

Thankfully, they don't completely have an aversion to vintage items, probably due to the influence from their parents.

You will see some millennials shopping at shows. However, it would take someone like singer and millennial Taylor Swift, who buys antiques for her homes, to announce in the middle of her concert that "Antiques are cool!" to make a big difference.

A Taylor Swift-signed 8 x 10 photo with COA (certificate of authenticity) is worth $200.

CHAPTER 39

On the Radio

For the fourth time, I was on Mike Ivankovich's Friday radio program called *What's It Worth*. This show is interesting because Mike always has guests to discuss the antiques or collectibles environment. Plus, he makes it fun for his listeners.

The first three times I was on his show, we spoke about particular genres of antiques and discussed values. On July 6, 2018, we discussed, "What is an antiques dealer today?" It was interesting and fun to do. The station covers the Greater Philadelphia area. Hopefully, Mike's audience for WBCB 1490 AM from 9:30 to 10:30 am will get something out of it.

The perception by some outsiders is that antiques dealers are people who deal in junk like Fred Sanford from *Sanford and Son*. However, we think of ourselves more like Indiana Jones discovering some precious incredible item.

An Indiana Jones "Holy Grail Diary" prop replica is worth $200.

Mike's program was enjoyable. He and I had good patter, and we conversed about how it's not easy being an antiques dealer. There are no regular paychecks, paid holidays, paid leave, or vacation time—no sick days, pension, or corporate ladder. It's a risky business, and sometimes you lose money on poor product investment. Product knowledge is everything. The more you know, the more you could possibly make in profit—or at least you hope so.

It's a risky business with every day being a treasure hunt. You may find something good at flea markets, shows, stores, yard sales, estate sales, someone's home, or online. But there are no guarantees.

Weather plays a big part in how well you sell at an inside show or outdoor market. Physical work is always involved because you are packing for a show or breaking down when it's over.

The upside is you can make your own hours. You schedule work when you want to or need to, and you decide how often you work. You can work around doctor's appointments, car maintenance appointments, children, and any other important engagements.

The one ideal I stressed on Mike's show was that as an antiques dealer, all you have is your reputation in this business. It's a smaller community than you think with cell phones and social media. Always tell the truth in your line of work and your customers will remember you for being honest.

It was the fourth time I was on his radio program. I called in from my home office. But this was the first time Mike called me after his show was completely finished to say how much he enjoyed the conversation we had on the air. It was a pleasure.

A 1930s Silvertone multiband shortwave tube radio is worth $85.

CHAPTER 40

The Late Great Sally Goodman

On August 1, 2018, after struggling from the result of a stroke in 2017 that left half her body immobile for almost the entire past year in a nursing home, Sally Goodman died after just turning eighty years old the previous month.

I first met Sally in the early 1980s with my friend George Massina when I was just getting acquainted with antiques. Near the end of the 1990s, my wife and our two daughters, who were toddlers at the time, loved browsing through Sally's store on West Ferry Street in New Hope, Pennsylvania. Her shop was floor to ceiling with quality antiques, and each room was decorated well. She carried almost every genre including sterling silver, Staffordshire, old copper, pewter, primitives, art, jewelry, textiles, and period furniture. All of her merchandise was perfectly displayed and gorgeous.

A nineteenth-century large hand-forged copper kettle cauldron, 14¼ inches in height, 17 inches bottom width, 21 pounds, is worth $300.

Sally was part of the old school of antiques dealers, yet unlike some older dealers who refuse to tell you any information about their antiques, Sally never shied away from answering any and all questions, which made me admire her more for being so forthright, informative, and honest.

Sally actually made discussing antiques exciting. Some experts give that pedestrian monotone lecture, but she was a joy to talk to and you just wanted to be a sponge and soak up all the information she had gathered over so many years. She doted on her little white dog, Emily, who loved to be scratched and petted—a real cutie pie.

It always bothered me that some old-school antiques dealers were afraid to tell what information they knew about antiques because then you would know too—as if it's a big secret because you'll make money from this knowledge and then they will lose income, which is so ridiculous and short-sighted. I felt, in agreement with Sally's philosophy, that if you told customers what you knew about an antique you might create a new collector who then goes out and purchases more of these items, which would be a win–win for both the dealer and the customer.

Sally joined the BCADA in the late 1970s when she called her business Sally Goodman's Frivolite. Her building was the historic Beaumont House, a Revolutionary War period home. She had quite the following with customers and was known as an authority on eighteenth- and nineteenth-century English and American antiques. She had clients in New York, Chicago, and California. Among the many antiques dealers in New Hope—and there were many years ago—she had one of the best stores.

Just across the river from New Hope, in Lambertville, Sally displayed merchandise in a second store that was a co-op. Her regular store also had an annex building next to it that carried mostly primitives and country furniture.

In New Hope, many antiques shops were folding due to the constant increase of the landlords' rent. However, it was not a problem for Sally because she owned the old beautiful stone building in which her store was kept. The store was in the front half of the first floor of her home. It was a close-knit community where the dealers would help each other any way they could.

After 9/11, many New Hope dealers were struggling, as were antiques dealers in general. They either retired from the business, moved far away, or died. Sally kept going but did pull back her hours to Saturday and Sunday or by appointment in her last ten years. She continually worked her store until she suffered the stroke.

Sally loved coming to the BCADA holiday dinner meeting and never held back her opinion on any subject. Although diminutive in size, she could be very tough but always fair and caring. She liked how I ran the BCADA show and liked me being president. When my father died, she couldn't have been kinder and deeply sympathetic.

Whenever I saw her smoking, which was often, I would implore her to "please stop smoking." Her response was always the same: "I know, I know." But she didn't stop until her mild heart attack in 2017 that later was followed up with the stroke. She left behind her two sons, Jason and Ethan, and her dog, Emily.

We had a thirty-second moment of silence for Sally at our September BCADA meeting. Then I said, "What I remember the most about Sally is when you knocked on her large heavy shop door, she would answer holding her little dog with a big smile that always meant 'Welcome.' I miss you Sally."

CHAPTER 41

The Pennsylvania Antiques Appraisers Association

I was approached in 2012 to become a member of the PAAA by the president, Dan Worden, who was my vice president in the BCADA at the time. After they analyzed one of my old appraisals as per their bylaws, I was voted into the club.

It's a relatively small group of about fifteen members, and we meet about six times per year. At each meeting, we initiate a "what is it," which is always fun especially when Stan Smullen, who is also a BCADA member, brought in an old sword from the Civil War. It was interesting to see how prices have either jumped or dropped over time.

An 1840 artillery officer's Saber with scabbard, made by the Ames Manufacturing company, is worth $11,500.

The PAAA website and brochure help market all the members' abilities, and I have received many interesting appraisal jobs through them.

One of my favorite functions as an appraiser is to perform a roadshow along with my colleagues Dan Worden and Ashley King. The three of

Dan & Ashley at Appraisal Day

us all have our own specialties and have become very close over the last few years.

Dan, known as The Silver Solution, has knowledge about silver, gold, other precious metals, dolls, Oriental, metal ware, china, furniture, and more. If you're not sure if a piece of silver is unmarked sterling or where it was made, Dan is the go-to guy.

A 1936 "Sir Christopher" pattern Wallace five-piece sterling silver tea set with sterling tray is worth $12,990.

Ashley, known as The Clock Trader, is an expert on clocks and watches based out of Quakertown, Pennsylvania. He spent more than ten years in Germany while in the Air Force. While there, he was educated by an old German man about clocks. Plus, he knows guns, tools, German antiques, furniture, jewelry, and more. If you need a clock or watch fixed, sold or bought, Ashley is the go-to guy.

A 1760 German Faience, tin-glazed earthenware tankard with a band-of-flowers decoration is worth $1,600.

My specialties include pottery, books, postcards, ephemera, American and European ceramics, collectibles, pop culture, sports memorabilia, artwork, metal ware, and more.

A pair of Leon Leyritz sculptured French Art Deco silvered bronze bookends are worth $20,000.

Between the three of us, we can do anything at a roadshow appraisal day. We have done many of them and people always bring something interesting or valuable. With all our different specialties, we usually satisfy everyone we see at these events.

We held an appraisal event at an assisted living facility in Princeton. Someone who saw the sign promoting the event walked in off the street. She brought in a document that her contractor husband had found inside the walls of an old building being torn down in Philadelphia. It was signed Benjamin Franklin with all the right curls he wrote at the end of his signature. We liked the look, the age, and the document itself, and we collectively felt it could equate a value of $30,000. The value also depends on the type of document that was signed. We recommended she take it to The Print Shop in Philadelphia to authenticate it. A representative from The Print Shop is on *Antiques Roadshow* from time to time, and they know their business. The woman was ecstatic. It's rare we find something this good at our appraisal events.

During an appraisal day at a church benefit, two strong gentlemen wheeled in a large, heavy twelve-arm crystal chandelier that had belonged to a relative. Everything was intact with no broken parts. It was electrified and quite beautiful. The fair market value in 2015 was $9,000. Today, it would be a slightly lower value. We applauded the guys for getting this immense heavy fixture into the building.

We had seen an early twentieth-century Royal Bonn green ceramic crystal regulator. This German piece is worth about $3,000. Ashley loves these and explained how rare they are. Royal Bonn made fine porcelain and earthenware in Bonn, Germany, from 1836 to 1921.

During one event at an art gallery in Somerville, New Jersey, we came across a beautiful nineteenth-century Swiss music box with all the wood in perfect condition. Condition is so important when determining value. We played it for our audience, and it sounded superb. The owner was happy to hear it was worth in the range of $3,500 to $4,000. Years ago, these Swiss music boxes were worth much more, but like so many genres in the antiques business, they are not bringing the value they once had.

A beautiful, large American Brilliant cut-glass bowl was only worth about $80 because the market doesn't find them desirable anymore. Years ago, it would have had a price tag of $200. This is the market today. It doesn't matter how beautiful or elegant the items are.

Most collectibles have taken a real beating. At an auction recently, a tray of six medium-size Hummel figurines sold for $40. That's for all six with no damage.

All Beanie Babies have dropped in value to just a few dollars each except one that is hot: the Princess Di Beanie, which comes in purple with a white flower on the chest of the bear. It sells for around $20,000 and was originally from 1997 as a first edition.

Lladro figurines in perfect condition, depending on size, are valued today from $15 to $100 instead of $45 to $300. These figurines are the best porcelain out of Spain.

Original Star Wars collectibles from the mid to late 1970s from the first three movies—*A New Hope*, *The Empire Strikes Back,* and *Return of the Jedi*—are hot. They will bring in hundreds of dollars over their original prices of $10 to $40. An Alec Guinness-signed box of the Obi Wan Kenobi figurine inside is selling for $1,600.

An interesting note: when George Lucas first showed a rough print of the first Star Wars movie later called *A New Hope* to distinguish it from the three later movie prequels, in the audience were his friends from film school—Steven Spielberg, Francis Ford Coppola, and Brian DePalma. DePalma directed *The Untouchables* and *Scarface*. It was DePalma who suggested, "Since I don't know who these people are and what they are doing, why don't you use the old movie scroll like in old serial films like *Buck Rogers* in the 1930s to inform the audience what's going on." That's exactly what Lucas did with the statement, "From a galaxy far, far away . . ."

Other hot items are musical instruments in good shape that are not pianos; they could be in the hundreds of dollars to thousands of dollars. Gibson and Martin guitars from the 1960s are selling for several thousand dollars. Pianos are difficult to move, therefore, on the secondary market values have dropped to double figures.

Metal lunchboxes from the 1950s and 1960s with thermoses and pop-culture names like the *Beatles* or television shows labeled on them could be worth up to $3,000.

Early twentieth-century lamps made by Handel, Pairpoint, and Fulper are some of the brands worth $4,000 to $40,000.

Early ornate glass Christmas ornaments through the 1940s are selling for up to $200.

Most of the time, we have seen items worth less than $40 at these roadshows. We try to make sure no one goes home crying because they thought they owned something they saw on *Antiques Roadshow*. When we see an item we think is interesting, we get the crowd's attention and educate the audience on what we found. At times, we pick an item that is a very good reproduction just to educate the public. You just never know what you might see. Dan, Ashley, and I always have a great time. Looking forward to the next one.

CHAPTER 42

Washington Crossing Card Collectors Club

Another group that I belong to and admire is the WC4, as we call ourselves. I joined back in 2006. It's a great group of people primarily from New Jersey and Pennsylvania, but there are members from other states and outside the country. The members are postcard collectors and dealers, otherwise known as the field of deltiology. The club is based at the Union Fire House in Titusville, New Jersey, where meetings are held once a month, usually the second Monday of the month at 7:00 p.m. There is an annual one-day postcard show on the Saturday after Memorial Day, also at the Union Fire Hall.

I learned a lot more about postcards from just being around the long-time members. There are specific people who help make the club move forward, including long-time member Betty Davis, who writes the club newsletter for those who can't attend the meeting or need reminders about dates. George Wagner is one of the officers, and as president, he runs the meetings and cares for the website. Heather Davis tirelessly takes care of membership dues. My good friend Sue Gettlen handles the Facebook page and runs a wonderful art gallery called Whispering Woods in Holland, Pennsylvania. She has assisted me in selling antiques. During each meeting, there is a postcard auction, and I am the auctioneer.

The real MVPs for this club are mostly the husband-and-wife team of Steve Cohen and Pamela Blake, who run the annual show with their minions and also help take care of all the minutiae needed to keep the club moving forward.

Postcards are one of the three largest collecting hobbies in the United States besides coins and stamps. Postcards are popular because of the wide range of subjects—anything can be on a postcard.

The first postcard in the United States was created in 1870. This started the "Pioneer Era" (1870-1898).

The first postcard printed for use as a souvenir included the twelve different designs of the buildings at the Columbian Exposition of 1893 and was printed on government postal cards. This introduced "picture postcards" to a receptive population. The cost was one cent instead of mailing a letter at two cents.

Until 1907, only the address could be written on the back of the card. These postcards had undivided backs, meaning they had no line down the middle of the back. That changed by law in 1907 to make it easier for the postman to read the address.

Postcard Periods

1870 to 1898: the Pioneer Era

1898 to 1901: the Private Mailing Card Era

Pre-1907: the Undivided Back Era

1905 to 1915: the Golden Age (which most collectors like)

1915 to 1930: the White Border Era

1930 to 1950: the Linen Era

1940 to present: the Chrome Era (these have glossy picture-type faces)

Postcard Sizes

Standard = 3½ inches x 5½ inches (the oldest cards)

Continental = 4 inches x 6 inches

Modern = 4¾ inches x 6½ inches

Oversized = mostly 5 inches x 7 inches and anything larger.

Postcard Types

Town views: exactly as it sounds

Sports: old, rare, can be valuable

Greetings: all holidays, with Halloween being the most sought after

Historical: including political

Art: special interest or art reproductions

Real Photos: valuable if it states a rare location, one that doesn't exist anymore, a famous person, or animals

What Makes a Postcard Valuable?
Age, Condition, Subject, Photo, or Postmark

Age: older postcards usually are more valuable

Condition: very important, no dog-ears in corners of card or writing on face

Subject: early train depots, early main street scenes, Halloween, catastrophes

Photo: details of a person's name or a place, wearing a uniform, children with animals

Postmark: a post office or town that no longer exists

Hottest/Fastest-Selling Postcards

1. Real Photo: Real photos from the early 1900s, if identified, including photos of children with toys, people with animals, sports teams, and local festivals. These types of postcards sell for $5 to $100 or more for rare ones.

2. Advertising: Images of banks, insurance companies, or products no longer there. These postcards sell in the $10 to $50 range.

3. Halloween: Most valuable "greetings"-type postcard. A postcard with an image of a mechanical African American child holding a jack-o'-lantern sold for $450. Regular Halloween postcards sell in the $15 to $90 range.

4. Christmas: Christmas postcards with Santa not wearing red sell in the $10 to $30 range. A postcard with Santa driving a car sold for $30.

5. Early Political: A postcard with an image of Teddy Roosevelt at a whistle stop running for office sold for $100 at auction.

6. Early Baseball Postcards: A Ty Cobb postcard sold at auction for $350.

7. Transportation: Early automobiles and zeppelins. An Austin Healy car sold at auction for $250.

8. Black Americana: The more detailed and racist these postcards are, the more valuable they are. These postcards sell in the $5 to $100 range. I have an African American client who buys these postcards. When I asked why he collects them, he gave me a great answer: "It shows how far we have come."

Postcards are an interesting field and with certain "paper" being hot sellers today, postcards are part of the mix within top-selling ephemera.

CHAPTER 43

Buying

The most important aspect as a dealer is not how you sell but how you buy. If an item is just too expensive to make a profit, leave it alone. If the owner of the item won't come down to give you room for a profit, walk away. It's not worth it; otherwise, you're going to live with that item for a very long time.

Remember, it's not how you sell; it's how you buy.

There are many places I like to buy merchandise. People may find you on various websites or selling at shows and they want to sell you their items. I do get an abundance of phone calls from people who find me this way, but often, I don't want what they have to sell. If it sounds interesting, I'll meet them somewhere or drive to their home. We come to an agreement on the price, and it's a win–win situation for everybody.

I attend many auction houses to attain more inventory. Some of my favorites are:

- Alderfer's Auction in Hatfield, Pennsylvania, 215-393-3000

- Brown Brothers Auction in Buckingham, Pennsylvania, 215-794-7630

- Robert H. Clinton Auctions in Ottsville, Pennsylvania, 610-847-5432

- Freeman's Auction in Philadelphia, Pennsylvania, 215-563-9275

- Tom Hall Auctions in Schnecksville, Pennsylvania, 610-799-0808

- Locati Auctions in Maple Glen, Pennsylvania, 215-619-2873 (online auction only)

- Kathy Mauer Auctions in Pottstown, Pennsylvania, 610-970-7588

- Joseph Pandur Auctions in Quakertown, Pennsylvania, 215-208-6481

- David Rago Auctions in Lambertville, New Jersey, 609-397-9374

- Renaissance Auction Group in Reading, Pennsylvania, 610-370-2879

These auction houses are honest, which is more important than anything else. You can view pictures on the auction house websites or use Auctionzip.com to find auctions with photos. You can place absentee bids if you can't make it the day of the sale.

There are also live online auctions that allow you to participate in the comforts of your own home. Alderfer's Auction has been conducting online auctions only on certain days of the month that do not conflict with their usual estate sale auctions. Alderfer's is a solid auction house run by CEO Sherry Russell and her hardworking, great team.

If you need to drive a long distance and find that the auction doesn't have enough merchandise you're interested in, then it's a big waste of gasoline, and more importantly, you wasted your time. It pays to view items online first before you drive far.

Buying at stores with reasonable prices can be lucrative. Some of my favorite local antiques stores in and around Bucks County, Pennsylvania, are:

- Antiques at the Old Church in New Hope, Pennsylvania, 215-794-5009

- Brownsville Antiques Centre in Trevose, Pennsylvania, 215-364-8846

- Bucks County Antiques Center in Lahaska, Pennsylvania, 215-794-9180

- Cook & Gardener Collections in Lahaska, Pennsylvania, 267-275-3933

- Dungeon Antiques in Quakertown, Pennsylvania, 267-490-9507

- Errant Artifacts in Quakertown, Pennsylvania, 267-231-9331

- Factory Antiques in Silverdale, Pennsylvania, 215-453-1414

- James Curran Antiques & Restoration, Lambertville, New Jersey, 609-397-1543

- Gratz Gallery & Conservation Studio in Doylestown, Pennsylvania, 215-348-2500

- Old Soul Antiques in Quakertown, Pennsylvania, 267-500-2134

- The Painted Shutter in New Britain, Pennsylvania, 215-340-0340

- The People's Store in Lambertville, New Jersey, 609-397-9808

- Quaker Antique Mall in Quakertown, Pennsylvania, 215-538-9445

- River Run Antiques in Point Pleasant, Pennsylvania, 215-297-5303

- 2nd Life Antiques in Quakertown, Pennsylvania, 215-536-4547

- Stone House Antiques in Mechanicsville, Pennsylvania, 267-544-0574

- Treasure Trove in Perkasie, Pennsylvania, 215-257-3564

- Zionsville Antique Mall in Zionsville, Pennsylvania, 610-965-3292

The aforementioned antiques stores are privately owned or multidealer co-ops.

I also find merchandise from stores in the Adamstown, Pennsylvania, area, which is sometimes called Antiques Capital USA. There are many shops here. My favorites are:

- Adamstown Antique Mall, 717-484-0464

- German Trading Post Antique Mall, 717-336-8447

- Mad Hatter Antique Mall, 717-484-4159

- Mother Tucker Antiques, 717-738-1297

- Renninger's Antique Market, 717-336-2177

- Shupp's Grove, 717-484-4115

- Stoudt's Black Angus Antiques Mall, 717-484-2757

There are many other stores. It will take you all day to browse if you are diligent, and you may find some excellent antiques.

The New Oxford, Pennsylvania, area is another hub with multiple stores that are worth seeing. They include:

- New Oxford Antiques Center, 717-624-7787

- Golden Lane Antique & Art Gallery, 717-624-3800

Another of my favorite places to buy antiques is the Cape May, New Jersey, area.

CHAPTER 44

Buying Antiques in Cape May, New Jersey

My family and I love to vacation in Cape May. It's our favorite of all the New Jersey shore towns. Our favorite place to stay is the Columbia Inn, where we usually rent the entire second floor when our daughters come down with us. My wife and the girls usually hit the beach while I go to work on the antiques hunt. I want to make sure I inspect most of the stores that I admire throughout the day. Then later, I meet up with the family for dinner.

Cape May has some great four-star restaurants where you may need to get reservations. They include:

- Panico's: great Italian food and seafood in an old former church

- 410 Bank Street: New Orleans-style food but not too spicy and great desserts

- The Merion Inn: great food and live music

- The Blue Pig Tavern at Congress Hall: elegant dining and great food

My family in Cape May

- The Ebbitt Room at the Virginia Hotel: farm-fresh food in an elegant setting
- Aleathea's Restaurant at the Inn of Cape May: great seafood and American cuisine with a beautiful view

A vintage wood "Fresh Seafood" sign, 24 inches long, in good condition, is worth $45.

There are probably twenty-plus antiques stores in and around Cape May. Some of my favorites are:

1. Cape May Antique Center: large co-op store with a mix of old and new; one of the biggest stores in Cape May area, 609-898-4449

2. Out of the Past: contains merchandise mostly from the early twentieth century to the 1960s; the knowledgeable owner once had a job riding the diving horse at Steel Pier, 609-884-3357

3. Antique Doorknob: great metal ware and furniture but expensive, 609-884-6282

4. Treehouse Antique Center: pretty two-story co-op with a variety of antiques, 609-884-4600

5. Antiques Emporia: has antiques mixed with new merchandise at reasonable prices; good military dealer here, 609-898-3332

6. West End Garage: co-op with antiques and vintage dealers; the building has been expanded to include more dealers and a refreshment area, 609-770-8261

7. Captain Scraps: on Route 9; I always find something here; good selection of antiques and vintage merchandise, fairly priced; will ship to your home, 609-624-1876

8. August Farmhouse Antiques: my favorite shop in Cape May area for years! Located in Cape May Court House, New Jersey; great merchandise; Larry and Arthur are BCADA members; great assortment and great stories about the merchandise, 609-465-5135

9. Ancient of Days Antiques: a series of small buildings detached from the owner's home; very good antiques mix; realistic prices; in Swainton, New Jersey, 609-465-9955

10. Treasure Past Antiques: one mile off Route 9 in Seaville, New

Jersey; large co-op with real antiques, worth a look; you can bring your dog inside the store, 609-624-2100

11. Riverbend Basket & Antiques: interesting store with good antique metal ware, ephemera, architectural items, artwork, and more; the owner, Patti Heisler, will work with you; in Tuckahoe, New Jersey, **609-432-5548**

A large primitive buttocks melon basket with tree branch handle, 20 inches tall and 15 inches wide, in good condition is worth $135.

CHAPTER 45

Selling

One of my favorite aspects of being an antiques dealer is selling my merchandise. I enjoy talking to customers to find out what their needs are, what they like, what they collect, and why they come to shows.

Many years ago, when I managed retail stores and today selling at shows and markets, I learned to always try to make sure my booth has an eye-catching display to draw attention to patrons. It is like the window display at a store, like I created in my younger retail days. Obviously, if more customers enter your booth, you have a better chance for more sales.

A 1906 brass and steel retail display rack, invented by Charles E. Schilling, 5 feet in height by 7 feet in width, is worth $150.

The show in which I have exhibited the longest is the Yardley Antiques Show. I've exhibited in this show since 1995. Ten years ago, I was loading my car on the morning of setup day for this show. In my garage, I removed a box that triggered some hanging snow shovels to fall, and I tried to catch them as they fell on me. A sharp edge from one hit me right on the inside of my left wrist where it bends. Blood starting bursting out as I ran in the house trying to find gauze and a large bandage without success. I had to use paper towels and duct tape to stop the bleeding and knew I needed stitches. This had to happen on show setup day—what timing!!!

Starting to get dizzy, I called my wife, Karen, who left her work and took me to the hospital emergency room because I couldn't drive while trying to cover my wrist with my other hand. When they took the makeshift bandage off, more blood gushed out. My wife had to leave the room from the sight. Each administrator, nurse, technician, and doctor kept asking me separately, "How did you cut yourself?" with their heads cocked to one side. It finally hit me that they felt I might be a suicidal person. When I explained what happened, it sounded so convoluted because the cut was perfectly centered on where the inside of the wrist bent. If I worked there, I probably wouldn't have believed it either.

The nurse needed to give me an anaesthetizing shot right where the cut was and told me it would only take eight seconds. A male nurse held back my shoulders because they were afraid that I might possibly hit the nurse giving me the injection. Twenty seconds later, the nervous nurse was still giving me the shot, and I was in the most pain of my life. They heard me scream throughout the corridor. I was not a good patient and very mad the nurse lied about the eight seconds. After a tetanus shot and several stitches later, we drove back home to get my packed car. Karen followed me with her car to the Yardley venue to help bring in my boxes. I wasn't allowed to bend my wrist or lift anything with that hand. Then Karen returned to her busy job. God bless my wife. Karen saved me, and the Yardley show was a success.

An antique surgical needle holder and scissors, circa 1900, are worth $70.

When you sell at any show or market, it's best to pay attention to your customers for a variety of reasons. By just saying hello when they enter your booth, it tells them you're available for any help they need, you're paying attention to their moves to prevent shoplifting, and you're the friendly face to answer a question. Many customers are introverted and are sometimes afraid to ask if they can't see it, "Can you tell me the price?"

By gently starting the conversation, you put them at ease. I've seen dealers do this and it works. When I was a teenager working at the Gap, the company drilled into us that retail means satisfying customer needs. You can't do this if you're sitting in a chair reading a book during a show or walking around checking other booths and leaving yours unattended. If you have an "I don't care" attitude toward your patrons, expect a terrible selling show.

Andrew Carnegie once said "Do your duty and a little more, and the future will take care of itself." This saying applies in sales as well. If you help your customer a little more than the usual, the sales will follow.

A 1913 signed Andrew Carnegie booklet titled How I Served my Apprenticeship as a Business Man *is worth $500.*

My friend and fellow BCADA member Scott Vombrack sold at the outdoor Madison-Bouckville Antiques Show in New York State. This long-running show is eight days, Sunday to Sunday. In 2018, it rained five of those days and was brutally hot on the others. People there didn't talk much. It seemed like everyone was self-absorbed. He said he really had to sell it. Therefore, when someone would enter his tent, he would say how much he liked their shoes or T-shirt just to get the conversation going. This tactic worked because he sold extremely well, while veteran dealers of this show said the gate was down by 10 percent. Scott can't wait to sell there again.

I have some wonderful regular customers at the Yardley Antiques Show. Some of them are with a local chapter of the Daughters of the American Revolution. They love anything George Washington. One woman told me when she arrives to the show, she heads straight for my booth in the lower back level of the basement. She always buys something from me. It's great to feel appreciated when you have a following, and you try not to let them down.

A pair of nineteenth-century George and Martha Washington silhouettes in tiger maple frames, measuring frame size at 10⅝ inches by 9⅝ inches are worth $250.

Be careful not to just carry merchandise that you love that may no longer be desirable today. A friend of mine who owns an antique store once said to me jokingly, "I have so many items I love that don't sell in my store. I may change the name of my business to 'Antiques Nobody Wants.'" Always mix up your stock with desirable items that you think customers are asking for.

The desirable 1950s set of four nesting Pyrex orange butter print mixing bowls are worth $375. Hard to believe!

About eight years ago on the last day of the Yardley Antiques Show, I sold a small oil-on-canvas painting, unsigned, of a beautiful young girl. A woman pushing a stroller asked me how much it was. I said, "Two thousand dollars for this late nineteenth-century original painting."

The woman said, "I live in Pennington (New Jersey), and I'll come back with my husband."

That's usually the kiss of death when they ask their spouse or significant other because they'll usually respond, "You don't really need it."

It was 3:45 p.m. and the show was closing at 4:00 p.m. I didn't think she was coming back. A couple minutes later, the woman showed up with her spouse and her baby in the stroller. She said to her husband, "It's beautiful. What do you think?"

The man said, "Whatever you want, honey!" and they bought the picture. I was stunned. It was a great way to end a show.

A 1928 Walter Emerson Baum oil on panel called The Red Barn, *16 inches by 12 inches, signed, in a gilt wood frame is worth $6,100.*

There was a remarkable story from 2009. A couple was looking at diamond rings from the dealer. He, tall and lanky, seemed to be on a mission. She was a petite and strikingly pretty blond. The man said to his girlfriend, "Which one do you love?"

The one she pointed to was the brightest sparkler in the box. Without asking "How much?" the man said to the dealer, "I'll take it."

Before the dealer could place the ring in a bag, the man grabbed the ring, assumed the knee position and asked the girl, "Will you marry me?"

She cried, "Yes."

That was one of the more amusing scenes I ever had to witness.

A vintage 14K yellow and white gold, single round illusion set diamond engagement ring, .13 carats, is worth $150.

You never know what people will buy. At the 2013 BCADA show, Old Dog Antiques exhibited eclectic items. They sold a train club car sink still partially attached to a wall for $150. One woman had to have it.

Old Dog Antiques once sold a beautiful nineteenth-century mahogany coffin with face window for $1,000. It was a real enticement in their booth and people were taking photos of it with their phones. Having an item to draw people into your booth is always advantageous.

Besides antiques shows, I enjoy selling at the Allentown Paper Show twice a year, in the spring and fall. It's run by a very steady manager, Sean Klutinoty, who will help you anyway he can. At these shows, it's not just antique ephemera for sale but any kind of paper. I usually bring books, postcards, prints, sheet music, bookends, posters, and sports ephemera. The bookends sell well here because people that buy countless books usually like bookends.

A pair of art deco nude dancer bronze bookends, 9½ inches in height, circa 1925, is worth $160.

I've done well at paper shows and learned a lot about what sells and what's dead. For example, circus posters are dying because—and this is hard to believe—too many people are afraid of clowns. Fear of clowns is called coulrophobia, and it's growing. Author Stephen King isn't helping either.

With Ringling Brothers/Barnum & Bailey circus going out of business due to lack of interest, the standard circus seems to be a thing of the past except for the Cirque du Soleil shows. They are a mix of acrobatics, music, and drama—still a hot ticket today.

A 1940s Cole Brothers Circus poster featuring "Betty Lou" (the chimp from the Tarzan movies), 201/8 inches x 27 inches, is worth $120.

At one Allentown Paper Show, a man asked me if I had any old TV Guides with Gene London in them. I said I didn't but gushed to the guy how much I loved watching his local children's television show as a kid, how much he meant to me, and that he made me want to read books more. He said, "Wait right here."

A few minutes later, Gene London was walking down the aisle toward me. I realized that guy must have been his assistant. My eyes welled up. Gene gave me a big hug and said, "I heard the kind words you said about me."

Gene was so gracious. We spoke for a while. I took a selfie with him. I love this guy.

A 1960s TV Guide with a Gene London story inside is worth $20.

At the Yardley Flea Market, once a year in September, sellers set up with their own tables and pay for the space. I take two spaces so I can have my car in my allotted area. All the money goes to the Friends Meeting House in Yardley. In 2017, my items were selling fairly well with my friend and fellow BCADA member Ted Freed next to me. I typically sell mostly $1, $5, and $10 items with the occasional $40 item as well. Ted sold a ton of this low-to-medium-priced merchandise and had a great day.

By early afternoon that same day, a polite lady was walking five large Labradors who were extremely well behaved. It begged the question, "Do all of these dogs belong to you?"

She replied, "Yes, to me and my husband. We rescued them from Puerto Rico during the flood."

I told her, "What a great noble thing to do." I had my picture taken with them.

An early twentieth-century sterling silver Labrador brooch, 36 millimeters in height, 9 grams in weight, is worth $100.

At a show where I exhibited, my neighbor and friend Jim sold an old brass tool to another dealer who also exhibited in a booth. That dealer had not paid for the tool yet. He waited until he sold the tool the next day and then paid Jim.

This is wrong and borderline unethical on a few levels. First, if you buy an item at the show, pay the dealer at that time. Second, after you buy it, don't place the item in your booth for the same show. Lastly, don't ever think of returning it because you didn't sell it at the show. Some people have no sense of ethics.

A vintage brass steam pressure gauge by manufacturer John Simmons is worth $160.

At BCADA shows, I'm more concerned that the show is running well, but I also try to make sure all customers in my booth are taken care of. In 2017, I actually had the best BCADA show ever dating back to 2010. People like to ask me what things I sell. The following is a list of what I sold from my booth at that November 2017 show: a Maxfield Parrish print, some Weller & Roseville pottery, Royal Bayreuth pieces, a pair of sailing ship prints, wood boxes, Nipper salt and pepper shakers, an original WPA charcoal drawing, a cast-iron eagle door knocker, Flow Blue china, an early Austrian pitcher, a rare Rowland & Marsellus pitcher, metal bookends, a Staffordshire bowl, a nineteenth-century George Washington litho, an early child's rocker with rush seat, an early rectangular glass paperweight with a photo of the first Ferris wheel, a Rowland & Marsellus curved-edge "Teddy Roosevelt" plate, a 1912 English Willow pitcher, a vintage dark oak set of drawers, a foot stool, a Hubley cast iron pig, a pair of Haines store bells, a pair of early school bells, and some other items. I was happy with the results.

An ornate Rowland & Marsellus Columbus Landing in America pitcher, circa 1910, is worth $250.

A large 18-inch-tall eagle cast-iron door knocker is worth $120.

A Flow Blue plate, circa 1860, "Pelew" pattern, is down to $50. The 1990s value was $110.

A Roseville vase, 7 inches tall, circa 1945, "Freesia" pattern, is down to $55. The 1990s value was $115.

A Maxfield Parrish print called "The Lute Players," large size, sold for $220. The 1990s value is $375.

Never talk politics while you're selling at a show. You will alienate many of the patrons, including some who may agree with you, because it's the wrong environment for such discussion. If someone tries to engage you in political talk, change the subject; it's not worth it. Discuss politics in the proper locale.

A 1912 Teddy Roosevelt Progressive Party pin is worth $335.

Selling is not an issue of "you either have it or you don't." It can be taught, and it's not that hard. Despite some people being introverted, it can be fun and you get to know your customer, as far as what they want and what they dislike. This knowledge helps you the next time you're purchasing for a show or for your store.

A 1786 Universal Magazine of Knowledge with leather dust jacket and copper engravings, published by William Bent, London, is worth $280.

CHAPTER 46

Downsizing and Selling Your Unwanted things

Whenever I teach a class about downsizing, it never fails that I see some people in the audience who have tears in their eyes because they don't know what to do with their late parent's valuable items or their children don't want their cherished possessions. I sometimes prepare appraisals for these people or at least help them find a way to unload their unwanted belongings.

I gave a presentation about downsizing to the Daughters of the American Revolution (DAR) Washington Crossing Chapter in 2018. The fifty or so people in attendance seemed to enjoy it, including BCADA member Helen Smith. Here it is below:

"My Kids don't want it". I hear this all the time from empty nesters and just about anyone who has children. So, how do you get rid of unwanted items? There are many options for you.

1. If you have an estate sale in your home, you need to price everything. People expect this and don't like having to ask. It won't take that long and is better for you in the long run. And make sure you have

plenty of help with the estate sale from friends or relatives for the sake of security. Spread all your help throughout the house, where customers are able to wander and browse.

For example, my friend had an estate sale without any help. Two partners who visited the sale surreptitiously stole all her good jewelry. They were eventually caught by police, but the jewelry was long gone and probably changed hands four times. She never recovered her jewelry.

2. If you do a yard sale, again, price everything for the sake of your customers. Many are so introverted; they may be afraid to ask for the price.

3. If a dealer says to you at a yard sale or an inside estate sale, 'I need a better deal because I'm a dealer,' then tell them, "You need to buy more items to make it worthwhile for me," or say, "Sorry, I think that's a fair price and I'm not giving it away." If they say, "Well, I'm leaving," LET THEM LEAVE.

4. If a dealer is buying multiple items, give them a better price because your ultimate goal is to rid yourself of the things you don't want.

5. If someone is coming to your home by themselves to look at what you have for sale, make sure you have someone else in the house with you. This is for security and so you are not bullied by your guest. Remember the person is your guest. If they say something you don't like, you can ask them to leave. This is another reason why you should not be alone.

6. Remember your gut feeling is usually right. If you just feel something is wrong, ask them to leave. If they want you to sign something to the effect that you are selling them your possessions, RED flags should go up. Don't sign anything. It's OK to say NO. Tell them, "I think your price for my items is unfair."

7. If you want an item appraised just to see its value before you sell it, use a certified appraiser! Remember an appraiser cannot accept payment from you in the form of merchandise. It is unethical. For example, if an appraiser says an item is worth $100, they charge $100 per hour, and they say they'll take the item as their fee, RED FLAGS should go up. How do you know the item isn't worth $500? Of course, this is different if a friend is doing you a favor and you give them an item to say thank you.

8. If you use an auction house to unload items, make sure you have a list of what you want to bring there because they will ask, "What else do you have?" Before they agree to a contract with you, they need to know what can they make at the auction. They spend the same amount of time on a $10 item as they do on a $500 item when they list your items for sale.

9. Auction houses usually get 15 percent to 25 percent on your items while you get to keep 75 percent to 85 percent. However, if they need to pick up large, heavy items from your home, then they will charge you for their time and gasoline to and from your home. All auction houses do this. If you're comfortable with their fees, sign their contract. That contract protects both you and the auction house.

10. The good auction houses that I like are Alderfer's Auction in Hatfield, Pennsylvania, Brown Brothers in Buckingham, Pennsylvania, Robert H. Clinton Auction in Ottsville, Pennsylvania, Freeman's in Philadelphia, Tom Hall Auction in Schnecksville, Pennsylvania, Joseph Pandur Auction in Richlandtown, Pennsylvania, David Rago Auction in Lambertville, New Jersey, Renaissance Auction in Reading, Pennsylvania, and Kathy Maurer Auction in Pottstown, Pennsylvania. These auction houses are all honest!

A January 12-13, 1995, rare Christie's New York Auction catalog featuring Nureyev and "Old Master Paintings," hardback with dust jacket, is worth $275.

CHAPTER 47

What's Hot and What's Not

Some examples of what's Not hot:

- Almost all glass: Depression, Cut, Pressed, Etched, Lead Crystal, Peach Blow, Satin, Crackle, Cranberry, etc. While glass has some value, it's not like in the 1990s.

- China sets, regardless of age or manufacturer—this includes collectible plates or souvenir plates. China sets are not appreciated by younger people because they mostly do not have dinner parties, therefore, no need for a set of china.

- Most American, European, and Japanese ceramics: vases, serving pieces, etc. While they have lost much value, more rare pieces will sell.

- Brown furniture: walnut, mahogany, especially dining room sets. See above about china sets. If there are less dinner parties then there is no need for dining room sets.

- Collectibles: Hummels, Beanie babies except "Princess Di bear" (which is all purple with a white flower, worth $20,000 in clear box), Cabbage Patch dolls, McDonald's tumblers, Precious

Moments (one of the biggest forced collectibles ever), LLadro figurines, etc.

- Old magazines: *National Geographic, Time, Look, McCall's, House Beautiful,* etc.

- Most Sports cards except Baseball cards older than 1950 with a star player. By the 1980's, manufacturers got greedy and printed too many, making cards less valuable.

- Anything Franklin Mint or Danbury Mint except for their value of gold or sterling if any. These mints would usually sell items as limited editions but they were forced collectibles not unlike Precious Moments. Today the Franklin Mint is out of business.

- Stamp collecting—it was once a big fad. Today, they are worth, if unused, the value on the stamp. Use them for postage.

- Hot Wheels & Matchbox cars once sold in the $100 to $200 range have dropped down to the $50 and less range. Still some value but much less.

Some examples of what's Hot (all in excellent condition):

- Movie posters with name actors like Cagney, Bogart, Karloff, etc. example: 1947 single sheet *Dark Passage* with Bogart & Bacall worth $2,500; 1950 single sheet *Sunset Boulevard* with William Holden worth $2,400. Note: difficult to find these in excellent condition because they are made of paper or linen.

- Mid-century modern furniture similar to what you see on the Dick Van Dyke show living room. This was mostly Danish modern décor. Some examples include a Milo Baughman flat bar chrome sofa worth $3,000 and a 1960s Hollywood Regency James Mont style pair of ottomans worth $2,000.

- Early lithographs or vintage items of George Washington, Abraham Lincoln, and Teddy Roosevelt. Some examples include a 1796 John Trumbull litho of George Washington worth $3,600; 1864 A.H. Ritchie steel engraving of Abraham Lincoln worth $1,200; and a Teddy Roosevelt kerchief made for the 1912 Presidential Campaign worth $2,600.

- Vintage yarn winders: $150 to $1,000 depending on size and age. Most houses owned these in the nineteenth to early twentieth century because most people knitted back then for their families.

- 1960 Schwinn bicycles: Apple Peeler, Orange Crate, Pea Picker, Lemon Peeler. Worth $2,500 to $5,000 depending on condition.

- French Baccarat Crystal Chandeliers run from $25,000 to $400,000 depending on size and detail. They hold their value.

- Petroliana (oil & gas items): 1930s Gulf Supreme Motor Oil sign is worth $2,900. However, the two guys on *American Pickers* are out of their minds buying bullet laced and very rusty metal signs and giving them extremely high values. That show is fake, otherwise, in a big warehouse of items, they would spend the entire episode in that one location.

- Black memorabilia like salt and pepper shakers or terribly racist early twentieth century postcards.

- Rare autographs of famous people. For example, Babe Ruth's autograph alone with certificate of authenticity is worth $35,000. Former Philadelphia Phillie Ritchie Ashburn's autograph alone is worth far less at $300 because he's less famous and because he signed everything, which decreases the value.

- Coin collecting is making a comeback! Especially those coins with silver or gold content. But not coins in jewelry—the attachment for that piece usually devalues the coin.

CHAPTER 48

The Spectacular 2018 show

On November 10 and 11, we actually had a better BCADA show than in 2017 with eight hundred patrons in attendance. I was ecstatic. The show looked impressive. Having quality dealers strengthens the show in many ways—perception of the patrons and notoriety spread throughout the antiques world.

At our last meeting of the year in December, I thanked all the exhibitors, setup crew, volunteers, members who pushed our show postcards, member and exhibitor Ruth Peckmann who paid for flowers at the venue, and anyone who helped make the show run smoothly. Everything clicked and made it a spectacular show.

Two tickets for the Radio City Christmas Spectacular featuring the Rockettes cost $360.

Patrons' comments were: "Great looking show"; "Love the mix of different antiques"; "I come here every year"; "Wish you would do it more than once a year"; and "Love the show, see you again next year."

August Farmhouse Antiques (Arthur and Larry) sold at the show for the first time and had a wonderful experience. They sold eighteenth-century Swiss sleigh bells, two pieces of furniture, an Arts & Crafts Period bell, and an 1810 Philadelphia coin silver sugar tong. Arthur is a certified appraiser, and Larry is a former interior decorator, making a great team together.

An Arts & Crafts Period bell, sold for $225, is worth $300.

Eighteenth-century Swiss sleigh bells, sold for $700, are worth $900.

The awesome and wonderful Julia Bartels of River Run Antiques who deals in holiday merchandise sold more Halloween items than she did Christmas merchandise. In fact, it was Julia's best show at this location, as it turned out for Pat Burke as well. Pat sold two Tiffany sterling pieces among other items.

New BCADA Vice President Lynn LoPresti of Hickory Farms Antiques had an excellent show—and she is an excellent officer in the club.

Jane Ashton, Benji Kidwell, Ted Freed, the Naylors, the Cheetys, the Abirs, Sherry Steigerwalt, Alan Snyder, the Rubens, the Frazers, the Spahrs, and Karen Taylor all sold well.

The Painted Shutter, with their usual outstanding-looking booth, sold considerably well. They also had a sale connected to the show the following week at their store in New Britain, Pennsylvania. Ivan Raupp of Magic Mettle Blacksmithing did well and sold a rare tool called a Twiddle.

A Twiddle, sold for $350, is worth $450.

The unsinkable Ruth Peckmann of Antiques in Bloom and Paula Foley of Foley-Carrow Art & Antiques both sold better than in 2017. Paula, a former museum curator, graciously speaks to her customers like she's giving a tour, and they are receptive. Paula always enjoys creating an eye-appealing booth and selling to her customers.

Gentleman Don Casto of My Turn Antiques had his best show in three years selling lead glass windows among other items. Cook & Gardener had their best BCADA show ever selling a World War II spyglass, an antiseptic sterilizer steel box, majolica, Minton, and other merchandise.

An antiseptic sterilizer steel box, sold for $350, is worth $450.

Marvelous Member Chair Doreen Dansky of Pentimento sold primitives and advertising well, including an Adirondack table.

An Adirondack table, sold for $150, is worth $300.

My sister from a different mother, Eleanor Jenitis, of ELtiques, had her best BCADA show ever selling lots of illustration art, many World War II letters, a 1939 New York World's Fair art deco lamp, and her usual ephemera.

A 1939 New York World's Fair art deco lamp, sold for $250, is worth $400.

New members Mary Ann and Grant Wyckoff of Roadrunner Antiques made the best of a large booth featuring many pretty antiques like rare Limoges china, original oil paintings, and other merchandise. More than any other exhibitor, they also had the most amount of show postcards come back to the show. Promoting the show with postcards is a big benefit to adding patrons to any show.

A 1915 real-photo postcard of an athletic show in excellent condition is worth $200.

I also received two phone calls from antiques dealers Teresa and

A Show booth

Jackie who visited the show just to tell me how good it looked and how much they enjoyed visiting.

Coming full circle, my childhood friend from Catholic school and a little frosty on top of his head, Sammy Marzulli and his lovely wife, Eileen, surprised me and visited the show from Philadelphia. It was their first time at any antiques show, and they loved it.

One of my regular customers, who buys a great deal of artwork from me, especially Philadelphia-related items, owns multiple homes. He sees me at many shows. On his way out of the building, he needed to inform me that it was the best-quality BCADA show to date, and I thanked him.

It was a great way to end the year.

A 1930s tin noisemaker for New Year's Eve with a picture of a woman wearing a strapless black gown and long black gloves including a man in the background, 8 inches tall and 4 inches wide, is worth $60.

Epilogue

The best thing about being a member in the BCADA is not just having your business listed on the website and in the brochure, listening to guest speakers at meetings, or exhibiting in the annual antiques show—it's the networking with so many honest, hardworking antiques dealers. The members educate you about merchandise and changes in the marketplace, becoming aware of new shows and new stores, and knowing about upcoming auctions. Networking with members makes you smarter.

Each year, I exhibit at about fourteen shows, sell about six times at the Golden Nugget flea market, participate in about five roadshows, handle individual appraisals, and teach several different antiques classes. It keeps me busy, and I still find the business to be engaging and fun.

I told my children after they completed college to please be a professional of some kind but not in my field. The antiques business is too volatile. Your paycheck is different from week to week. Get a job with a constant salary, benefits, and paid holidays and sick days.

Thankfully, my two daughters listened. My oldest, Emma, has a great job working for a medical publishing company. Julie has a college degree in accounting and will follow in her mom's footsteps.

It's daunting to write about your family and friends. What do you keep in, and what should you leave out?

In my life, I have admired so many people I have met over the years in the antiques business and outside the business. I think by following their lead, I have become a better person. I learned a lot and shared a lot, and I don't think I would change a thing. The best antiques are old friends!

An 1885 first edition hardback of Personal Memoirs of U.S. Grant, two volumes in gilt-decorated green cloth, is worth $174.

March 2019

Acknowledgements

I need to thank those people who read parts of early drafts and gave me helpful advice including Patricia Burke, Doreen Dansky, Paula Foley, Ted Freed, Mark Bindelglass, Sherry Steigerwalt, Scott Vombrack, and of course, my editors, Frank Levy and Tina Brown.

I am also grateful to members of the Bucks County Antiques Dealers Association; members of the Pennsylvania Antiques Appraisers Association; members of the Washington Crossing Card Collectors Club; The Catholic Youth Organization; Our Lady of Consolation; The Police Athletic League; The Council Rock Renegades; The Book & Record Exchange and the Newtown Bookshop in Newtown, Pennsylvania; Central Books and the Doylestown Bookshop in Doylestown, Pennsylvania; Farley's Books in New Hope, Pennsylvania; the city of Philadelphia and all their sports teams; Cape May, New Jersey; the Gardenville Hotel; the Golden Nugget Flea Market; the Washington Crossing Inn; the PSPCA; the BCSPCA; and the Fab Four.

My parents who I miss dearly.

All of my teachers and mentors who made a difference.

All my friends and relatives who I love so much including those no longer with us.

My kids who make me proud, our dog Nicky who makes me run, and my wife, Karen, who gives me direction.

If anyone's name is left out who helped me over the years, I ask your forgiveness.

Bibliography

www.1stdibs.com

www.abebooks.com

www.antiquescapital.com

www.askart.com

www.BCADAPA.org

www.BucksCountyAlive.com

www.capemay.com

www.cupboardsandroses.com

www.facebook.com

www.homeandantiques.com

www.invaluable.com

www.mlb.com/Phillies

www.P4A.com

www.paappraisers.net

www.raabcollection.com

www.rubylane.com

www.thefest.com

www.tias.com

www.tripadvisor.com

www.trocadero.com

www.upscalejunkandantiques.com

www.VisitNewHope.com

www.visittacony.com

www.wc4postcards.org

CPSIA information can be obtained
at www.ICGtesting.com
Printed in the USA
BVHW050537160819
555912BV00002B/1/P

9 781977 214362